HAWAIIAN HERITAGE PLANTS

by

Angela Kay Kepler

Published by The Oriental Publishing Co.
P.O. Box 22162, Honolulu, Hawaii 96822, U.S.A.

Printed by China Color Printing Co., Inc.
229, Pao Chiao Road, Hsintien, Taipei, Taiwan, R.O.C.

ISBN 0-932596-21-5

TABLE OF CONTENTS

Acknowledgements 4

Approaching Hawaii: the carpeting of an archipelago 6

'Awa 11

Bamboo ('ohe) 17

Banana (mai'a) 22

Coconut (niu) 27

Wild Ginger 32

Ferns: False Staghorn (uluhe) 35

      Maidenhair ('iwa'iwa) 38

      Sadleria (ama'uma'u) 40

      Treefern (hapu'u) 43

Hala (pandanus) 46

Hau 49

Hibiscus, red (kokio-'ula) 53

Hibiscus, white (kokio ke'oke'o) 56

'Ie'ie (climbing screwpine) 58

'Ilima 64

Ironwood 67

Koa 69

Kukui 74

Lobelias (haha) 80

Maile 84

Mamane 86

Mango 89

Morning Glory, seaside (*pohuehue*) 92

Mountain apple (*'ohi'a 'ai*) 94

Beach Naupaka 97

Noni (Indian mulberry) 99

'Ohelo 104

'Ohi'a 107

Olona' 112

Poppy, Hawaiian (*puakala*) 115

Pukiawe 118

Sandalwood (*'ili-ahi*) 122

Silversword (*ahinahina*) 129

Taro (*kalo*) 134

Ti 137

Wauke (paper mulberry) 141

Wiliwili (Hawaiian coral tree) 145

About the Author 149

Wind-blown hala: *indispensible in old Hawaii.*

K. Kepler

K. Kepler

*Black-flowered cyanea (*Cyanea atra*), a lobelia.*

ACKNOWLEDGEMENTS

Native streamside vegetation, Haipuaena Gulch, Maui.

R. Hobdy

Koli'i, *a stunning lobelia (*Trematolobelia macrostachys*).*

I would like to express thanks to numerous people who have contributed in varied ways to the making of this book. Bob Hobdy and Derral Herbst taught me much Hawaiian botany and were always a delight to be with in the field. The U.S. Fish and Wildlife Service granted me opportunities for visiting remote corners of our islands. All those who shared pouring rain, biting winds and scorching sun, shared tents, drove me over terrible roads, flew me in helicopters, fixed vehicles, checked my whereabouts with radios, or otherwise hiked with me, I thank sincerely for their company, encouragement and knowledge.

Librarians (State and Maui Community College) were extremely helpful in locating unusual or rare off-island books. Thanks also to those who allowed me to use their color transparances to augment mine: Dave Boynton, John Carothers, Bob Hobdy, Marie McDonald and Bill Mull.

Those responsible for land access permits, newspaper editors who originally ran earlier Maui versions of these chapters as weekly columns (Ron Youngblood and Nora Cooper), and others who proofread or helped in other ways (especially Ed Bryan, Wesley Wong, The Nature Conservancy) are also gratefully acknowledged. Ron Lester freely shared his expertise in design and layout.

Lastly, I wish to acknowledge the early training from my parents and teachers, and the more recent good behavior of my children, Sylvelin and Leilani. This book would not have been possible without the indispensible aid and encouragement of my husband Cameron, who not only provided opportunities for field work, but proofread the manuscript, assisted with photography and contributed companionship and stimulation both in the field and at home.

To all, my heartfelt thanks.

APPROACHING HAWAII:
CARPETING AN ARCHIPELAGO

The Island of Hawaii as a bird might have spied it eons ago.

> *"Darkness slips into light*
> *Earth and water are the food of the plant...*
> *Water that caused the withered vine to flourish*
> *Causes the plant to develop freely*
> *Multiplying in the passing time."*

from The Kumulipo (Hawaiian Creation Chant)

Sitting in a jet flying 33,000 feet over the Pacific it is hard to imagine any living thing being able to survive outside the window in that cold and inhospitable environment.

While building a sandcastle a child picks up a freshly fallen orange fruitlet from a *hala* tree and momentarily plays with it.

In late summer flocks of shorebirds appear. You see them feeding or flying around in groups along the shore, wading in ponds, probing mudflats or congregating high in mountain pastures.

Air currents high in the sky, ocean currents swirling around our coasts and migratory birds arriving from all points of the compass all have one thing in common. They are the principal means by which plant seeds arrived in Hawaii eons ago.

Our islands are the most isolated land areas (of any appreciable size) in the world. They lie more than 2,000 miles from North America, Alaska and Japan, about 5,500 miles from the Philippines, and over 2,000 miles from our nearest major

*rain forest fern (*Dryopteris parallelogramma*).*

Survival is hard for the a'e *(*Polypodium peliucidum*).*

island group to the south, the Marquesas. Over millions of years lava spewed out from the depths of the ocean to create islands and natural forces shaped them into magnificently contoured forms. At the same time plant seeds descended upon these oceanic oases from every direction. They came purely by chance, alone, and always under extremely rigorous conditions.

A handful of miniscule fern spores leave the safety of their protective parent plant and are thrust into the air by a tropical storm in Malaysia. Winds swirl furiously, whisking them in all directions; some fall to germinate in the coziness of their preferred surroundings; others drop into the salt water to perish.

Several spores, however, are drawn skyhigh to enter a fast jet-stream of freezing air at 35,000 feet altitude. This rushes them towards the central Pacific Ocean. On the way some are whirled higher into the upper atmosphere to disappear, but as the winds approach Hawaii one seed enters a slow branch stream. By sheer chance it drops down into Oahu's developing wilderness rainforest and, despite the fact that it has been frozen, miraculously thaws and begins to grow.

It was a very lucky spore. Billions of other spores and seeds of all kinds succumbed to the trip's numerous hazards. In fact, only about two percent of Hawaii's plants arrived by air currents.

Then there is the ocean route. Take *hala.* Everyone knows the attractive *hala* trees, with their tufts of twisted leaves, multiple "prop" roots, pineapple-like fruits and bright orange fruitlets that drop to the ground. If you pick up one of these fruitlets you will note that the freshly fallen ones are very fleshy. As time passes, this pulp dries out leaving a tufted end like a coarse, stubby paintbrush, and a dry, lightweight portion at the opposite end. When you submerge the whole fruitlet, tiny bubbles of air become trapped in its fringes, allowing its tiny seeds to become encased in a cork-like, bouyant "life-jacket".

To colonize our shores, dried *hala* fruitlets bobbed up and down like corks in calm and stormy seas, totally at the mercy of complex currents. Eventually they

An emergent, volcanic, stream-eroded island; a welcome sight for stray birds. (West Maui Mts. from the south.)

Because 'ohelo's ancestors were attractive to they are now available to us too.

Hala *fruits on a woven* hala *mat.*

K. Kepler

Hala germinates right in salty coastal lava.

Many cloud- or avian-borne seeds drop into wilderness areas such as this remote valley on Molokai.

C. Kepler

were thrust up onto sandy beaches or thrown mercilessly over jagged lava rocks.

Approximately one-quarter of our native plants have descended from ancestors that survived these incredible journeys. Most had clever flotation devices.

And lastly, what role did birds play in seed transportation?

Imagine a shorebird such as a Ruddy Turnstone feasting on a stock of 'ohelo-like berries located on some far-off South Pacific Island. While returning to Alaska to breed, an unusual storm blows it eastwards to Hawaii, many miles from its normal migratory path. Miniscule undigested seeds in its innards are spurted out in a dropping after the bird alights. If these seeds land in the right type of soil in a suitable area, and if the climate, elevation and other conditions are appropriate, they might grow.

Actually, a seed transported by birds stands a better chance of survival than one subjected to the whims of winds and waves. This is reflected in the proportion of our native plants that arrived in this manner – almost one-half.

These ideas may seem a bit far-fetched, but they are true. Seeds *did* arrive, although admittedly the processes spanned millions of years. Countless numbers perished en route, and many that endured the journey clinging tenaciously to their tiny sparks of life shrivelled or rotted because they landed in the wrong places at their final destination. Those precious few that survived evolved into one of the most fascinating and unique collections of plants in the world.

It has been estimated that approximately *one* successful immigrant every 50,000 years could account for the known Hawaiian flora! The extreme isolation of our island chain resulted in the fact that a remarkable percentage – 98% – of our 3000 or so native ferns and flowering plants are found nowhere else.

Then seeds and seedlings accelerated their speed of arrival. Approximately 1600 years ago Polynesian men first set foot on our shores. They, like birds, brought plants with them. And they, like pioneer plants, were faced with a predominantly alien environment.

Through centuries of familiarization with Hawaii's natural history, these people developed a fine subsistence culture, blending the utilization of their own introduced plants and animals with those already here. A wealth of knowledge accumulated as each generation verbally transmitted information relating to food, medicine, transportation, fishing, weapons, crafts, clothing, games and religious ritual. In addition, taboos (*kapu*), folklore and poetry intertwined themselves with everyday practicalities.

Since these remote times, Hawaii's shores and mountains have been considerably reshaped by Polynesians, whites and Orientals with their attendant animals, fire, diseases and constantly increasing multiplicity of plants, the natural forces of vulcanism, climate and her timeless, encircling ocean.

In this book I have attempted to weave cultural and biological, historic and geographic, aesthetic and spiritual aspects of Hawaiian ecology into non-technical accounts of selected plants, both native and introduced. It is my fervent hope that these discussions, spanning pre-Polynesian Hawaii to the present, will contribute to an ever-deepening endearment for, and a desire to help preserve, these island gems that we are priveleged to inhabit.

Most cloud-borne spores and seeds perish as winds and rain plummet them into the ocean.

'AWA

-sided, shady valleys such as this occasionally harbor an 'awa shrub.

If we reflect upon the history and habits of societies, both ancient and modern, we find that people have always used intoxicants, stimulants or sleeping potions, and they have always worshipped divine powers greater than themselves. Often the two were inextricably linked, molding the character and cultural essence of the people concerned. What worlds apart are the fiery Scots with their potent whisky, the meditative American indians with their soothing tobacco, the Mexicans with their consciousness expanding mescalin, and the carefree Polynesians with their muscle-melting, soporific *'awa*!

In Polynesia, *'awa* roots provided the staple intoxicant and prepared a route (for a small percentage of the population) to the nether world of spirits. In Hawaii today a bewildering array of stimulants, alcoholic beverages, drugs and meditation techniques are available if we choose to enter states of inebriation or superconsciousness. Until haoles arrived with liquor and methods to distil *okolehao* from *ti*-roots though, *'awa* was the main substance available. (*Ti*-root "beer" was not as popular.)

Drunk primarily for its intoxicating, sleep-inducing pleasure, *'awa* was enjoyed by all classes of people, especially royalty. In early Hawaiian history *'awa* was taboo to commoners, but by the mid-19th Century there was plenty for everyone.

K. Kepler

A young "green 'awa" plant.

Harvested 'awa stalks, unfortunately not replanted.

Men planted it around taro patches, beside mountain streams and in forest clearings. They also collected it in abundance from the lush lowland forests where it had escaped from cultivation. As with several other Polynesian-introduced and native plants, though, it was exploited mercilessly and is now extremely rare.

Some Hawaiian chiefs, whose lives were primarily devoted to eating and drinking, were addicted to 'awa, downing several cups each day between their enormous meals. Often in semi-drunken stupor, their skin flaking off, their eyes swollen and bloodshot and their bodies helplessly inactive, they presented miserable, unkingly specimens of humanity to western visitors.

Hard-working farmers or fishermen could not afford the time to sit around all day, even though Polynesians in general did not toil as ardently as European or Oriental peasants. After a full day of rowing, bending, digging or sitting on the edge of a canoe, 'awa was a welcome relief from the strains of physical exertion. Its soothing, relaxing effects enabled them to face another day of the same activity. For the *kahuna* (priest) 'awa was an indispensible aid in medicines, ceremony and "black magic". For example, while treating a person who had contracted an illness as a result of offending an ancestral guardian, 'awa was a necessary offering. Whatever the religious ceremony – invoking spirits at séance, "praying a person to death", or the weaning of a child – 'awa played a prominent role.

Not any type of 'awa was permitted either: at least 15 varieties had their particular uses. The most esteemed was "sacred black 'awa", reserved for the most important occasions; the most common was "green 'awa".

Thus royalty drank for pleasure, the working class for relaxation after labor, and the *kahuna* for religious and ceremonial reasons.

'Awa was so special that each family reserved specific cups to hold its bitter brew. Simply carved from coconut shells, they constituted one of the few items made in old Hawaii from these potentially invaluable containers. In other Pacific cultures elaborate bowls and cups were (and still are) similarly reserved for 'awa, for example the enormous Fijian *kava* (*yangona*) bowls that measure several feet in diameter.

Traditionally 'awa root was chewed and spat into a communal bowl. Preferably the chewer did not salivate copiously, although the enzymes in human saliva were considered beneficial, converting 'awa's starches into palatable sugars. Water or coconut water was then added and the murky, fibrous mixture strained and squeezed through sedge stems. When the cups were filled a prayer of gratitude was offered to the gods, thanking them for their blessings and requesting a good life in this world and beyond. Hawaiian ritual was very simple compared to the elaborate formalities required in more equatorial islands, although naturally this varied with the occasion and host.

The general drinker was not a light and merry tippler: his primary aim was intoxication, and the quicker it happened the better. He did not sip his 'awa as if it were a delicate wine with a subtle bouquet! He held his breath, gulped the whole lot down, then grabbed a stick of sugar cane, fish or sweet potato to offset its bitter taste. If the first cup did not make his eyes see double, he continued until his head gravitated downwards and his legs dissolved beneath him. A full night's profound sleep ensued, after which he supposedly awoke completely refreshed.

As in all cultures – Germans and British come immediately to mind – there were heavy drinkers who took pride in the heavy doses of 'awa that their bodies could tolerate. Years of boasting (and consequent addiction) unfortunately manifested in both mental and physical disorders, especially when 'awa was mixed with alcohol. The following 19th Century accounts represent typical descriptions of Hawaiian overindulgence of 'awa:

"The appearance of purely animal gratification on the faces of those who drank it, instead of being poetic, was of the low, gross earth. Heads thrown back, lips parted with feeble sensual smiles, eyes hazy and unfocussed, arms folded on the breast, and the mental faculties numbed and sliding out of reach."

"I observed, that the chief's skin was very rough and in scales, resembling somewhat the shell of a small terrapin" (tortoise).

'Awa reminds me of the oft-quoted Biblical passage, "Take a little wine for thy stomach's sake". In small quantities relaxants are not harmful, but excessive intake can lead to serious consequences for individuals, families and society as a whole. Although obviously a potent drug, 'awa's occasional use is probably alright, but

The rare, sacred "black 'awa", greatly esteemed by Hawaiians.

K. Kepler

13

Typical habitat for shade-loving 'awa.

K. Kepler

extreme usage in Hawaii produced many sick, indolent people and incapable leaders. It led to overconsumption of alcohol and its attendant problems which still persist today.

An Hawaiian woman bears a still-born child. Instead of burying it the couple decide to present it as an offering to their family deity, the celebrated shark-god Kamohoali'i. Placed upon a red tapa mat, with auspicious offerings (*'awa*, taro, sugar cane), the child is thrown into the ocean. The parents trust that its soul will transmigrate into the shark's body and forever more protect their family from future shark attacks. A ceremony at the local temple follows, complete with additional *'awa*, black pigs, taro and coconuts. At sunset and sundown the *kahuna* addresses more prayers to the idol representing Kamohoali'i, at which time he covers himself with water and salt. As this mixture dries his skin becomes scaly resembling both a shark and an *'awa* drinker. The priest then wraps himself in red tapa, utters piercing shrieks and leaps around proclaiming to the parents that he has just been revealed the exact time when the child's soul entered the shark.

Such was a ceremony observed by the French explorer, Freycinet, in the late 18th Century. It was one of the many instances where *'awa* root was believed to exert potent influences upon the ancient Hawaiian gods.

'Awa was a special offering, not only because the people *felt* it was sacred, but because they were sure the gods themselves would enjoy it, as they did. In some respects their gods were conceptualized as "super people", living in a far away

"heaven" and heeding the people's repentance by granting blessings, increasing harvests from land and sea, providing innumerable babies and so forth. They also warded off misfortunes such as diseases, epidemics and sudden disasters. The closest symbol of 'awa's divine protection in our present culture is "holy water." Botanically, 'awa is a most attractive shrub, growing to about 15 feet high. It is related to the black pepper that we sprinkle daily on food. 'Awa grows best in damp shaded valleys at fairly low elevations. A few localities on each island were famous for their 'awa groves, for example Puna (Big Island):

"Most potent this 'awa of Puna!
It wafts the seduction to sleep,
That I lock my senses in sleep!

'Awa's large, heart-shaped leaves have gracefully curving veins resembling those of yams, while its heavy, jointed stems are reminiscent of bamboo. The portion preferred for making the famous beverage is the "root" (actually an underground stem), which forms a knotted mass several inches thick and up to two or three feet long. The larger the 'awa root, the better the quality, for the root evidently concentrates strength and flavor with passing years. If at all possible, 'awa drink was manufactured from fresh roots, although in these modern days where convenience products are universal, instant powered 'awa is acceptable even in the remotest villages of Fiji! Fijians, who export 'awa powder, still use it regularly; any small occasion is a prime excuse to haul out the *kava* bowl and have a party.

Personally I have not tried 'awa root, but those who have (including my husband, during a Fijian ceremony) tell me that it's taste is unpleasant, acrid, pungent and rather "muddy". Your mouth and tongue become numb, then your muscles completely melt as you enter a euphoric state where you are fully conscious but cannot speak. 'Awa acts first on the central nervous system and muscles and later (only if drunk to excess) on the brain. Friendliness dissolves into slumbering tranquillity.

Medicinally 'awa has been used in many Pacific cultures. Natives of New Guinea used it as a pain-killer while tattooing and Hawaiian "medicine men" prescribed it to alleviate ailments of the head, muscles, bladder, reproductive organs, skin and for general debility. A leper on Molokai recounted to me that once, after several week of severe nerve pains, fiery flashes over his entire body, and numerous sleepless nights, he tried a little 'awa as a last resort. Its marvellous anaesthetic effect provided him instantly with a full night's sleep and daily release from the agony that only lepers understand.

Believe it or not, one of Hawaii's earliest export items was 'awa root! Although slow-growing, it was cultivated on the Big Island and Maui. Rights were granted to local people to collect the roots for personal use and expensive permits were required if the 'awa was sold. It was decreed (sensibly) that every person was to plant two dozen cuttings for every mature plant removed. (Whether people did this or not is a moot question, as today hardly a plant can be found anywhere, and those whose secret spots are known are cut down mercilessly.) The industry folded after 14 years, having exported an estimated 15,000 lbs. Pharmaceutical laboratories in Germany were the main buyers, where biochemists used it for medicine and analytical research. The demand for fresh 'awa dwindled as some of its active ingredients became synthesized artificially. (Incidentally, three of these ingredients have appropriate names: kawain, dihydrokawain and methysticin, all based on the Polynesian variant of *'awa, kawa,* and its scientific name, *Piper methysticum.*) However, *'awa* is not completely relegated to the dust-shelf of history. In Hawaii, people from a large cross-section of society, from local senior citizens to haole Ph.D's enjoy a little *'awa* on the side. Many old-timers who do not have access to it now recall pleasurable moments of its past effects too. Mrs. Young, an elderly Big Island lady and grand-daughter of King Kalakaua, states that today a green *'awa* extract is dehydrated and used as a relaxant for astronauts traveling in outer space! Thus it has survived from primitive sorcery to our present space technology.

 'Awa, an attractive plant, and a definite part of Hawaii's history, is today a very rare plant, even in Hawaii's remotest valleys. Its modern equivalent, *pakalolo* ("pot"), planted in similar semi-cultivated fashion in forest clearings, has usurped its place!

Scientific Name: Piper methysticum
Other names: *'awa* (pronounced "arva"); *kava, kawa, 'ava, yangona* (other Pacific
 names)
Family: Piperaceae or pepper family; about 1200 species; related to black pepper,
 peperomias.

Two native forest relatives of 'awa *(*Peperomia *spp.).*

B
A
M
B
O
O

Typical bamboo forest (with hala *on left), feathery and green.*

Bamboo. Mere mention of the name evokes associations with Oriental cultures and people. Contemplative Buddhas sitting in peaceful bamboo thickets, rare pandas munching on tender bamboo shoots, elaborate bamboo dwellings and fences, or the staggeringly complex scaffolding surrounding Hong Kong's high-rises. Over one thousand uses have been tabulated for this remarkable "grass", cousin to corn and sugarcane.

In its usefulness it rivals, perhaps even exceeds, the coconut palm, creeping into every facet of living in both traditional and contemporary Asian countries. From intricate Japanese tea-whisks to foot-wide irrigation flumes, its products embrace an astonishing range of practical and esthetic usages: food, housing, transport, medicine, games, weapons, art and ornamentation.

Bamboo was a late-comer to Hawaii. Even though approximately 1,000 species occur naturally on every continent except Europe, with species native to the Pacific, it never reached Hawaii without man's aid. Its sprouts were carefully carried here by Polynesian voyagers and, as is usual for Polynesian-introduced plants, the actual date of introduction is unknown.

According to legend, the old Hawaiians were fully aware that it was not native to their adopted archipelago. The great gods Kane and Kanaloa reportedly planted now historical groves, and Goddess Hina also transported bamboo from far-away Tahiti, planting it beside her door. In all probability bamboo *did* come from Tahiti, as "Hawaiian bamboo" (*'ohe Hawaii*), which grows wild on lower slopes and in valleys, is an Asian species also found on other Pacific islands.

Bamboo flourishes best in our warm, moist forests, perpetuating itself by underground runners which send up sprouts near, or many feet from, the parent plant. Bamboo rarely reproduces itself by seeds as do most other flowering plants.

Its flowering is fascinating. Each species flowers after a fixed number of years which may be as little as one or as many as 120! Huge sugarcane-like flowerheads appear, become laden with seeds, then the whole grove dies. It takes years before the few underground runners that survived, along with fallen seeds, fill out the original grove again. In some types, according to Japanese authorities, *all* plants, wherever they are growing in the world, flower simultaneously. What a wierd phenomenon... can bamboos communicate telepathically? What are the advantages of groves in, say Hawaii and Thailand, flowering at the same time?

Certain bamboo stands in the Hawaiian islands are renowned for their antiquity. Of interest to Maui residents is the fact that Hina's original grove was on Maui's windward coast, where today (in Waikamoi) extensive areas of several types of bamboo grow. Other famous groves are at Hilo and along the Puna coast (Big Island), and near Kaunakakai (Molokai).

The old Hawaiians used bamboo, naturally, but never foresaw its potential as fully as the Asians, who had lived with it for centuries. Its degree of use depended on the amount available and its proximity to villages. Bamboo provided miscellaneous items such as water containers, fishing poles, irrigation troughs, knives, design stamps for decorating tapa, and musical instruments. Medicinally it was insignificant; slivers of sharp bamboo performed circumcision rites, and bamboo ashes were used in concoctions for curing skin sores – a real paucity compared to the elaborate Chinese pharmacopoeia.

I find the musical instruments most interesting, mainly because two of the three types are still used. The *pu'ili* or bamboo rattles (I believe unique to Hawaii) consist of a section of bamboo from which one cross-piece is removed, and the hollow section beyond it split into numerous fine divisions. When shaken or struck, these spaghetti-like strands rattle against one another as air passes through their filaments, producing, as Emerson describes, "a breezy rustling sound". Depending on the nature of the hula performed, bamboo rattles were either shaken lightly, clashed forcefully or tossed deftly between partners. Such dancing was light and trivial rather than profoundly religious.

Nose flutes (*'ohe* or *hano*), although lost traditionally from Hawaii, are occasionally encountered in the Pacific today. Pierced with only two or three holes, this narrow "flute" was stopped by the fingers of one hand, supported by the fingers of the other hand, and blown with regulated breath through one's nostril. They

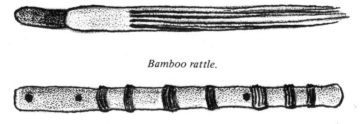

Bamboo rattle.

Nose-flute.

obviously possessed a limited musical range and a thin, wheezy tone, but recordings from French Polynesia possess a captivating, almost ethereal sound emanating from these primitive instruments.

In Asia bamboo has always been regarded with immense respect. Almost every temple houses bamboo brushwork inside and living bamboo outside. In Japan especially, it is associated with high spiritual values. The haunting notes of the clarinet-like *shakuhachi* are calculated to transport you to high spiritual realms, and bamboo is a must for the New Year's symbol of happiness.

In old Hawaii bamboo was useful but not special. Apart from the belief that it was planted by gods and goddesses, there is no evidence that it was attributed any particular respect. Over the last century though, Oriental people have added a richness to bamboo's Hawaiian heritage by superimposing their cultural uses and beliefs gleaned from long exposure in their homelands.

Smooth jade-green columns rustle and clatter in the half-light beneath a pale green, feathery canopy. Occasional bursts of wind cause the air to vibrate within open bamboo columns, and pure flute-like notes resound through the thicket. What primaeval sounds... nature's own spontaneous music!

It is July in a bamboo forest on Oahu. If you look closely you will see an old Chinese man, bent over and moving slowly between the hundreds of closely spaced stems. For many years he has come to this area, collecting edible bamboo shoots as they emerge in early summer. He snaps the stout shoots off at their bases and with a sharp knife, peels away most of the fibrous sheathing. It doesn't take him long to collect six onion bags full, after which he returns to his battered World War II jeep, brushes aside the ever-present mosquitoes, packs the bulging sacks, and drives back to Honolulu.

His wife awaits him at home. Under a large starfruit tree they further pare the shoots and split them lengthwise. Both are delighted a at the good haul and anticipate many scrumptious meals using this traditional Oriental delicacy. A big fire is blazing and soon pots of

Smooth, shiny, jade and yellow-green culms tower skyward.

K. Kepler

shoots and salted water are bubbling merrily. Next day, after soaking the shoots several times, they are ready for canning in glass jars. The experience of gathering this bounty from their island and of being in touch with one of the Orient's most special plants, engenders to them inner warmth and satisfaction. Besides, store-bought shoots imported from Japan are very expensive! They recall "the old days" when local factories canned and sold bamboo shoots very cheaply.

As far back as 1000 B.C. the Chinese people, experts in many fields of know-ledge, recognized bamboo as a type of grass. They were right. Today its jointed, hollow stems (culms) and characteristic stem-sheaths, leaves and flowers, place it within the enormous grass family, together with sugar cane, Job's tears, oats, barley, corn, and garden pests such as crabgrass and kikuyu. Unlike trees, which increase in girth over many years, new bamboo sprouts emerge at full diameter. Also unlike trees, which have solid trunks, bamboo culms are divided into a series of open tubes separated by woody cross-pieces. Such unusual anatomy inspired the old Hawaiian riddle: "A calabash (container) and a cover, a calabash and a cover until the heavens are reached." The answer, naturally, was bamboo.

The Hawaiians too, knew its botanical affinities. They named it 'ohe, a general term that included all types of bamboo plus several bamboo-like plants and grasses.

Bamboos are remarkable plants in many respects. As well as their outstanding utility, their growth rates are phenomenal, unsurpassed in the entire plant kingdom. Once, in Kyoto, Japan, a bamboo sprout increased *four feet in 24 hours*! That translates to two inches every hour, a pace reminiscent of speeded-up movies depict-ing motions of flower growth. A giant bamboo of Indomalaysia, an enormous "grass" with stems up to ten inches in diameter, has been similarly known to reach its 100 foot height in a mere two months!

Ornamental bamboos may shoot up and spread relatively fast too, quickly be-coming uncontrollable, as many gardeners can attest. Once their sturdy runners become healthy, they have no regard to sending up shoots in "proper places"; they may pop up in such unlikely spots as the neighbor's lawn or the middle of your asphalt driveway! (P.S. Concrete is the answer to your dilemma.)

Our wild bamboos are popular for fishing poles. A wise fisherman knows the length, diameter, shape, and wall thickness that is best for the type of fish he plans to catch. "Hawaiian bamboo" is the most readily available, but there are better types if you know where to find them. For example, on Kauai a stocky, thick-walled bamboo is unsurpassed for *aku* (a type of tuna) fishing.

Surely one of the most pleasing aspects of bamboo is the smooth shininess of its culms, giving them beauty, strength and flexibility. Run your fingers up and down a section of bamboo; large diameter pieces are best. You feel the woodiness, yet it almost seems as it a silicone coating has been applied to the outside. This is due to silica deposits within its stem. If bamboo is correctly steamed and dried, this firmness and luster will persist for many years. For example, well over 1000 years ago a suspension bridge was constructed in central China using thick twisted bamboo cables that function to this day! If bamboo is improperly treated however, it mildews and rots fairly quickly.

Bamboo's silica enables fresh culms to hold a sharp cutting edge, a fact which was appreciated by ancient Hawaiians. In the absence of iron and large clam shells, obliquely-cut bamboo provided their best knives and daggers. Thus they supple-mented their stone adzes and small shell-cutters with bamboo, slicing through every-thing from umbilical cords to cooked pig's thighs.

After 1900, especially during war years, when supplies were restricted, Hawaiians of many backgrounds untilized bamboo for such diverse items as woven hats, kitchen utensils, houses and canoe outriggers. Foresters planted it to prevent soil erosion and maintain watersheds, and businessmen contemplated making paper from it, as is still done in the Orient.

It is easy to see bamboo in the Hawaiian islands. Almost any lowland road in the wet (windward) regions of the Big Island, Oahu, Maui or Kauai will eventually pass through a grove. Hikers should be rewarded with small groves up moist valleys and almost all botanical gardens and arboretae grow several species.

Today bamboo is a small but valuable forest resource; its uses reflect the influence of several cultures. It enhances and preserves our countryside, highlights our gardens, provides edible delicacies such as *loompia*, catches fish, inspires painters and lends a special charm to those who spend time within its elegant confines.

Scientific Name: Common bamboo, *Bambusa vulgaris*
Family: Graminae or grass family, about 4,500 species, related to corn, sugarcane.

A fresh bamboo shoot, bursting with vitality .

K. Kepler

BANANA

One day in the early 19th Century, two young chiefesses, Kapiolani and Keoha, were feeling dejected and defiant. They could not understand why women were forbidden to eat so many foods that looked and smelled delicious: bananas, coconuts, pork, turtle and many kinds of fish. Even living in high-ranking, royal families, their diet was rather monotonous, consisting primarily of poi, sweet potatoes, yams, *limu* (seaweed), certain fish and taro tops. On special occasions they savored dog and chicken and also picked mountain apples and *akala* (raspberries) in season. It wasn't fair though. The village had plenty of bananas, and even common men ate them. Yet if any woman was caught eating one she was immediately sentenced to death. (Actually, women were allowed to eat the *iholena* and *popo'ulu* varieties, but they were rarely given any.)

Why? No-one seemed to know, but an old *kahuna* (priest) told them that Wakea, the revered ancestor of all Hawaiians, had declared them forbidden. The banana tree was to be respected as an embodiment of the great god Kanaloa, who had supposedly brought the first plants to Hawaii from "Kahiki", his ancestral homeland. Religious observances were strictly observed, and if bananas were to be offered as sacred foods at the temple altars, then women, inferior beings, must go without. Perhaps, the girls surmised, there were not enough bananas to feed everyone and the gods too, so ladies have had to suffer ever since.

With a mischievous twinkle in her eye, Kapiolani separated the folds of her skirt momentarily, revealing one of the golden-skinned, contraband fruits. She beckoned to her friend to follow her to the ocean, where they hid behind some rocks, stripped off the peels, and shared the smooth, creamy, sweet flesh.

Very few crimes escaped undetected, and this one did not either. A sharp-eyed *kahuna* spotted them, reporting their transgression to higher authorities. Due to their royal rank they were absolved from the offense, but someone had to be blamed, so their tutor was drowned. (Incidentally, Kapiolani later became a High Chiefess and christian, once defying the Goddess Pele by eating *'ohelo* berries, which led to the legal abolishment of all Hawaiian gods. Right from childhood she must have questioned the validity of certain religous customs.)

In observing the conventions of people from diverse cultures (including our own), an outsider has no trouble in finding illogical rules and odd behavior. The rigid taboo (*kapu*) system of old Hawaii was no exception. It complicated the lives of natives and foreigners immensely until its abolition in 1818. Seemingly useless restrictions, such as women not being allowed to eat food cooked in the same utensils as that for men, or even from the same underground oven, are difficult to comprehend. Women could not even partake of food with their own husbands or infant boys after weaning! Any infraction of these laws plunged families into mourning and misery.

Bananas, mentioned in Indian manuscripts from Buddha's time (600 B.C.) have been cultivated and enjoyed by inhabitants of every warm country in the world. The traditional Hawaiians were, I believe, the only people possessing stringent regulations upon their consumption; certainly no other Polynesian culture did so. Even menehunes, the tiny, cheerful, industrious, mythical people who lived very early in Hawaii's pre-history, are reported to have lived in houses built of banana leaves, existing primarily on bananas and fresh-water shrimp, so there was no taboo then.

These wonderful fruits were staple items in the diets of all Pacific dwellers; indeed, the South Pacific Island banana plantation is still a way of life for thousands of people today. Each part of the banana plant is serviceable – leaves, trunk, sap, terminal bud and flowers. Leaves especially are employed for every conceivable purpose: rainhats, design stencils, tablecloths, bowl-covers, temporary mats, dyes, plates, cigarette papers etc. In the Micronesian-Philippine area people even wove delicate fabrics from the fine, silken fibres stripped from the leaves of a large species of Asian banana.

Anywhere in rural areas, if you stop to pass the time with a villager, he will as often as not grab a nearby knife and lop off a couple of banana leaves for you to sit on. Before long you are sipping fizzy coconut water and munching starchy baked green bananas.

Wild bananas on sea-girt cliffs.

Standard daily fare customarily includes these plainly cooked bananas; however, on festive occasions the culinary ingenuity of our southerly neighbors shines. In Fiji, for instance, green bananas and taro are grated, mixed with coconut cream and baked; a more recent Tahitian "poi" recipe blends ripe bananas, papayas, taro, pineapple and coconut cream into a sumptuous dessert.

It is interesting to compare the extent to which certain plants are used throughout the Pacific. All Polynesians, Micronesians and Melanesians possessed common ancestors and traditions, yet during many hundreds of years of isolation, each island group evolved its own unique life-styles, customs, beliefs, and plant uses. This depended a great deal on available resources. On small islands, banana plants, for example, were utilized in hundreds of ways that never appeared in Hawaii, where the banana's importance was overshadowed by a greater variety of other plants. Banana fiber is fine for strings, netting and baskets if you don't have anything better; Hawaiians had the strongest fiber in the world, *olonā,* a native plant, so bananas were not used much for threads and ropes.

This is not to say that the people of old did not use bananas; their importance for survival was just minimal. Imagine a wedding day, say, at Hanalei on Kauai. You would find people carrying rocks and banana trunks towards a large earthen pit, already partly filled with slashed banana stumps, an important source of steam. Others would be preparing the food for this underground oven (*imu*): a pig wrapped in banana leaves, fish enveloped in *ti*-leaf casings, packets of taro and sweet potatoes. After these were put in, men would place banana leaves, old woven mats and dirt over the succulent mound to further hold in heat and generate more steam for the several hours of cooking that lay ahead. One man would be likely to haul away a couple of banana trunks to use as canoe-rollers, and perhaps an old lady would wander off with a gourd full of banana sap for incorporation into a tonic.

It is impossible to generalize about the way Hawaiians grew bananas. In moist or irrigated areas, men grew them in small clumps near their huts and on dykes adjacent to their flooded taro terraces. During excursions into the mountains, they planted *keiki* (young ones) along streams and in flat pockets of soil where rainfall was high. Such plants, multiplying naturally, served as emergency rations, and many of their descendents still exist as "wild" patches today, reflecting some of the areas favored by Hawaiians.

We have some evidence that bananas were better cared for on the Big Island. Archibald Menzies, botanist on Vancouver's ship (1792-1794) wrote glowingly of the Kealakekua plantations: "... we entered the wood by a well-trodden path, on both sides of which were luxuriant groves of plantains and bananas reared up with the great industry in the neatest order of cultivation."

Undoubtedly why bananas did best on the Big Island is because they are essentially tropical plants, and this island lies closest to the equator.

Internationally speaking, the banana was, and still remains, one of the world's most useful plants. Dyes, alcohol, fruits, medicines, clothing, bags, nets, cattle fodder and wrappings are a few of its multitudinous uses in tropical countries. On account of the many superstitions surrounding bananas in old Hawaii, its uses here were limited. It is difficult to imagine a culture with bananas playing an important role when women were not allowed to eat them, and it was considered ill-luck to even encounter a person carrying a bunch!

"The Great Banana!
The Great Banana!
It will yield ten hands!
The bunch cannot be carried,
It will take two men to carry it
With difficulty."

This exclamation, expounded forcefully while lifting a banana *keiki* high into their air, was believed in old Hawaii to contain magical powers. A banana plant was regarded as a person, a symbol of man. Because of this, it was important for a planter to make the correct postures and gestures. Otherwise the plants would not bear productively. In addition, there were a plethora of rituals and beliefs, such as the right time of day, phase of the moon, and supplications to the god who protected all banana plants, Kanaloa.

However, despite the care given to many plantings, either in protected valleys or beside a taro terrace, there were times when, as now, no amount of careful attention could prevent their banana patches from being ripped apart.

In Abraham Fornander's "Hawaiian Folk-lore" are stanzas indicating that gales and furious storms have descended upon our islands from time immemorial:
"The fierce wind as the rumbling of thunder in the mountain...
Moving to cause damage, the mischievous wind
Tearing up bananas and leaves of trees....
Nothing remains through the destructive march of the wind....
The banana leaves come floating down....
The sign of that fierce, relentless wind,
Devastating the forest."

Despite the hardiness of banana plants, they need care to bear well: a large hole, good drainage, mulching (the Hawaiians used ferns and banana plant "trash"), and nitrogenous fertilizer are necessary, especially during the fruiting period. And plenty water.

Banana plants may look sturdy, but they are actually about 80% water!. It comes as a surprise to most people that bananas, although attaining 30-40' in height, are not technically trees at all. They do not have a trace of woody material. Their thick, succulent trunks consist entirely of fleshy leafbases overlapping one another, so that in cross-section all you see is a set of watery concentric rings, looking like a huge onion.

Incredible amounts of water are required to bring a banana plant to full maturity – on average, about *16 feet of water per year!* It is no wonder that Hawaiians utilized nearby streams to water their banana patches. And it is no wonder that the first plants in your garden to blow over when furious storms whip through your property are your bananas, generally top-heavy ones laden with fruit too. Water is not as strong as wood!

In the Hawaiian language we find two appropriate sayings relating to this point. *Nui pumai'a ohaka oloko* translates as "It is as large as a banana stem, but soft inside." In other words large, but not strong. The second carries the same theme. *He pumai'a, loa'a i ke kikaio:* "He is like a banana stalk, but falls when hit by a gust of wind." This is a remark deriding someone for appearing strong, but when a test arises, he cannot help but show his weakness.

The banana has a fascinating life history. Planted as a *keiki* a couple of feet high, it soon replaces its narrow juvenile leaves with large rounded blades. Each new, tightly-rolled leaf grows upwards from a shortened, ground-level stem, aided by a white waxy lubricant. When the plant is mature, with an attractive spreading crown of numerous broad leaves, this small stem lengthens and pushes its way up through the sheathing leaf bases forming the trunk. This central column then bends over, opening to reveal the smooth, terminal, purple "bud", which is a marvellous protection for dozens of little yellow flowers that will later develop into fruits.

Each group of flowers is protected by one purple, leaf-like covering, which rolls back like a rose-petal, exposing it to the outside world. Without fertilization, the many flower-bases become transformed into baby bananas, which begin as tight bundles, fitting together snugly. As they grow, they push apart and fill out into the familiar round bananas. The plant must then be cut down, as it only bears fruit once.

A hiker washes wild iholena *bananas in an adjacent stream.*

Today hundreds of varieties produce a myriad of banana shapes, sizes and textures, colors and tastes. They may be short, long, bitter or sweet. Their flesh color ranges from dirty white through various shades of yellow and orange to pinkish-salmon. Many are delicious raw; others require cooking. If you have a chance to sample a "wild Hawaiian" banana, it will most probably be the *iholena* type, with apricot colored flesh (best cooked) and bronzy undersides to the leaves. Most banana types can be cooked before ripening, giving an unusual, gelatinous texture, which a creative cook can turn into exotic dishes with the addition of vegetables, proteins and spices.

Hawaiians in past eras considered bananas so special that they were occasionally presented to the gods as prime offerings, along with humans, pigs, 'awa and coconuts.

Speaking as a woman, I'm extremely grateful

Tubular flowers develop into luscious fruits.

that those beliefs are abolished today. Not only can we all share the delicious tastes of many types of bananas prepared in numerous ways, but we can enjoy them at the same table with our husbands and male guests, even serving them from the same platter!

Scientific Name: Musa paradisiaca
Family: Musaceae or banana; about 125 species; related to plantains, bird-of-paradise, heliconias (lobster claws), traveler's palm.

Banana flowers maturing into fruit. Note how the flower shrivels as the fruit enlarges.

C
O
C
O
N
U
T

Germinating coastal coconut.

One of the tallest and most beautiful palms in the world and certainly the most utilitarian of all trees, the coconut is a symbol of the tropics. With hibiscus flowers and alluring brown-skinned women as allies, this proverbial palm has enticed millions of tourists, adventurers, artists and residents to tropical shores.

In many senses, this graceful tree IS the Pacific. Without it, people would probably never have undertaken their historic voyages across uncharted oceans, and surely would not have colonized low-lying atolls. Pacific history would have taken completely different turns and been far less colorful than we know it today.

Simply stated, the coconut represents life itself. Inhabitants of many islands cannot live without it and cultures on many larger islands developed such a dependency on it that their lifestyles today still reflect deep-rooted associations with it. In addition to the widespread coconut-and-fish subsistence, there are many recorded instances where, during droughts, coconuts provided the only drinking water available for months. In times of severe hurricanes, people have even lashed each other to strong, flexible coconut trunks in order to avoid being swept out to sea. Coconuts have saved the lives of many stranded persons, providing food, water, materials for shelter and shade from the merciless equatorial sun.

For those who have been priveleged to touch such cultures, even briefly, one views the coconut with respect and wonder. To the ancient Polynesian, their great gods created the coconut palm, the "tree of heaven" as a loving gift to man. Naturally, all across the Pacific, legends have attempted to elucidate the mystery of the palm's origin. Essentially they speak of a beautiful girl, Sina, who falls in love with a young man named Tuna. They are forced to part. Tuna changes himself into an eel and swims to Sina's home village, where he is killed. As he lies dying, he asks Sina to bury his head and from it will grow a tree that will provide all that her people need. If Sina becomes thirsty she can husk its nut, thereby exposing two eyes and a mouth, Tuna's face. She can drink the sweet water from his open mouth and kiss her lost lover at the same time! Romantic, yes, but it symbolizes more, I think. The coconut and eel were both forms of a loving and all-providing god common to many cultures.

Hawaii forms a remarkable contrast to the rest of the Pacific; the coconut, though used occasionally, was never an essential element of Hawaiian culture. For example, weaving from its leaves was not a common practice; in fact, the leaves were not used for much except simple fans and temporary shelters. How different from islands to our south, where even today rural people live in coconut thatched huts with side-walls made from plaited coconut fronds, weave coconut baskets, and make string, fishing floats, toys, brooms, platters, bowls, snares and flower arrangements from various parts of the coconut frond!

Utilization of coconut meat (copra) is the major occupation on such islands. Family life revolves around products of these lovely palms: people eat vast quantities of coconut "meat" at different stages of maturity; drink the sweetish, transparant coconut water from the green nuts; ferment the flower sap into a maple syrup-like "toddy"; squeeze coconut cream from the grated copra for mixing with vegetables and fish; use nut milk and embryo in baby foods and medicines; and rub fresh oil into their skin.

One talks to modern housewives in Hawaii about how they use coconuts growing so prolifically in their yards, and the answer is inevitably that coconuts are a nuisance and too hard to open. Repeat your question on less developed Pacific islands and you'll receive much more varied and ecologically sound replies. A Fijian will describe a creamy pickle made from the gelatinous young "spoonmeat" and red hot peppers; a Tahitian or Cook Islander's eyes will sparkle as she talks of the delights of raw fish, onions, lime juice and coconut cream. A Samoan will describe how she mixes coconut oil with bamboo leaf ash and applies it to soothe burns. In Tarawa (Kiribati) a villager might recall how coconut water was used as a replacement for blood plasma in transfusions during World War II.

The ancient Hawaiians, even though refusing to allow their women to eat coconut meat, knew that it was worth their while to open coconuts. Fishermen chewed and spat the meat onto the surface of the ocean, knowing that the liberated oil would smooth out wavelets and produce a calm gloss that enabled them to spot fish better. Before shampoos arrived in Hawaii, people soaked their hair in masticated copra, thus replacing lost hair-oils and producing shiny tresses.

During the 19th Century, after the taboo on coconut eating was lifted, people drank coconut water more frequently and ladies experimented in the kitchen, creating "recent traditional" Hawaiian foods. The most famous of these is *haupia*, a thick pudding made from coconut milk and sugar, thickened with arrowroot or cornstarch. Other delicacies include mixing coconut milk with grated sweet potatoes, taro, chicken or greens. (Coconut is nutritious too, containing calcium, phosphorus, iron, proteins, and vitamins B and C.)

Over most of the Pacific, coconut husk was (and still is on

Coconuts beautify the City of Refuge, Is. of Hawaii.

C. Kepler

remote islands) the primary source of fiber. Separated and rolled, coconut sennit was used for everyday jobs for which we would use thread, string, rope, nails, tape or yarn. Not so in Hawaii. Hawaiians, as well as having coconut sennit to work with, were lucky to have a wide selection of other fiber plants too: *olonā*, in

Coconuts and South Sea islands are conceptually inseparable. Pago Pago Harbor, American Samoa.

particular, was their favorite as it was much more versatile. Coconut sennit (*'aha*) was nonetheless useful. Being coarse, it was used where ropes of strength and durability were required, for example, in house construction, where each pole and cross beam was carefully lashed to another in a typically Polynesian figure-of-eight fashion. Almost all Hawaiian weapons (of which there were quite a variety) utilized sennit. Shark-teeth swords (used for disembowelling enemies), tripping weapons, daggers, slings, and clubs all possessed sennit straps. If canoes needed to be caulked, men soaked coconut fibers in breadfruit sap and inserted them into cracks and crannies. The fibers strengthened the breadfruit glue, thus preventing water from seeping in.

The reason why coconut fiber is so strong, so durable, and so resistent to seawater relates to the reason why it exists in the first place! After all, it is just a heavy overcoat for the coconut seed, enabling it to float over vast expanses of ocean. Drop a coconut in water. Despite its heaviness, it floats. Air-spaces between the fibers and within the nut itself provide bouyancy. After about four months of floating, a coconut is still able to germinate, although it may take over a year to do so.

As we have mentioned before, Hawaii does not enjoy a truly tropical climate, and this may be our clue as to why the coconut palm was not too important here. Our archipelago is relatively "cool", centering around 20° N. It also benefits from the tempering influences of high mountain air and the north-east tradewinds. In the heart of Polynesia, closer to the equator, coconuts have always flourished; the trees there are more robust, healthier and more productive than those in Hawaii. On the margins of Polynesia, on islands such as Hawaii and Pitcairn Island, the coconut assumed a lesser role in living, and in temperate New Zealand they died out altogether. Let's face it: coconuts don't like the cold! Your cannot even grow them here above about 2000 feet elevation.

Despite all this, coconuts do quite well in coastal areas, especially on the most southern tip of the Big Island, the point closest to the equator. Hawaii's climate therefore does not adequately explain why they were not planted more extensively, nor why women were forbidden to eat the nuts. This is a real enigma, as our initial settlers came from a culture which utilized coconuts extensively. Some unknown time after they took up residence here, taro became their staple, their life and their love. It replaced their traditional coconut. Perhaps the reason was simple: Hawaii's native vegetation provided practically nothing for people to eat, and taro, owing quicker than coconuts, was the first substantial food that could keep them

Drying copra (coconut meat) for export, Western Samoa.

K. Kepler

alive. It takes a coconut palm eight to ten years to bear nuts in Hawaii, and this was too long to wait!

After changing island homes, their all-providing gods conceptually altered from those who provided everything from the coconut palm to those who supplied basics from more varied sources. The Hawaiians ended up living in grass-thatched huts, subsisting basically on taro, weaving primarily from *hala*, using containers fashioned from wood and gourds, and concocting medicines and dyes derived from a much larger selection of plants.

Complex vegetation and life-zones, characteristic of large mountainous islands, provided many options for the basic needs of their inhabitants. The old Hawaiians therefore evolved a different and more varied life, far removed from their cousins on smaller, lower islands where the coconut was of paramount importance.

Today a revival of interest in coconuts has begun in the form of imaginative palmfrond weaving, and who does not enjoy "chicken *luau*" and *haupia* at parties? Don't be afraid of coconuts, just because they are hard! Get out your hatchet. With a few blows and judicious pulling, the nut splits open. (You don't need to tear off the husk unless you want to keep the shell.) A few cuts with a small knife and prying with a screwdriver and lo, all your coconut meat is out. Eat it plain as a snack, blend or grate it for freezing; or slice it thinly, marinate in teriyaki sauce and bake for scrumptuous hors d'oevres. To make coconut milk (the basis of curries, desserts, drinks or main dishes), merely whiz the coconut meat in your blender, add boiling water, and strain through a thick dish-towel. Then, if you have a fireplace, burn the husks!

My husband and I once talked to some rural villagers in Western Samoa about the United States, and they provided us with a fresh perspective on their native traditions relating to coconuts. We spoke of highways, multi-storied buildings, huge populations and many other features of American life. They were surprised, but not amazed. But when they asked us about our coconut plantations, and we told them that many private homes and organizations hired men to cut down the nuts before they ripened, so they would not fall on people's heads, they stared at us incredulously. "You cut down unripe coconuts? What kind of society do you live in?", they queried. To them, the ultimate societal degradation was to destroy that which kept people alive. And for us to have no recourse to alternative food-sources originating on our own islands after destroying fruits from the coconut palm was absolutely unbelievable. What would happen if your ships and airplanes didn't arrive?

And besides, they finally laughed, EVERYONE knows that coconuts never fall on the heads of good men anyway!

Scientific Name: Cocos nucifera
Other names: niu, nu, ni (Polynesia)
Family: Palmae or palm; about 2,700 species.

...namental coconut sepal "roses".

Trimming coconut palms in Hawaii – a sacrilege elsewhere in the Pacific.

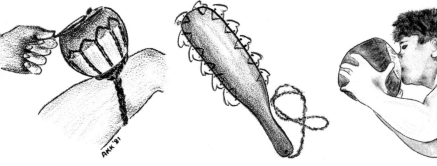

Coconut shell knee-drum.

Shark-tooth weapon with coconut sennit string.

Drinking fresh coconut water.

What would the tropics be like without a "coconut palm sunset?"

WILD

GINGER

Former taro terraces, now clothed with wild ginger.

Like graceful swans upon a calm lake, Liana's smooth supple hands glided smoothly but firmly across her husband's bronzed back. She dripped a little more fragrant lubricant from a small nearby calabash into her hands and continued massaging. To each set of muscles she gave individual attention, squeezing or kneading them.

She had spent several hours that morning preparing her massage "oil", derived primarily from the *'awapuhi* or wild ginger plant. First she had pounded a few of its "roots" (actually thick horizontal stems) with some fresh sandalwood flowerbuds. This was then mixed with the clear aromatic slime which exuded from the reddish, cone-shaped flowerheads of the *'awapuhi*. After straining this sweet mixture through natural fibers, all was set.

While out collecting her ingredients, she brought back extra materials from all parts of the perfumed plant. One sister used the flower slime for shampooing her hair. She squeezed the copious liquid over her long black tresses, using it first as a shampoo then later as a conditioner to add luster. Even today, one of the vernacular names for this plant is "shampoo ginger". I love its smell and occasionally use it in combination with a commercial shampoo.

In traditional Polynesian manner, Liana's father used the *'awapuhi*'s leaves to flavor meats and fish while they baked in the *imu* (underground oven). *'Awapuhi* "roots" had a variety of household uses too. Women sliced, dried and pulverized them, then added the scented powder to large calabashes containing folds of *tapa* (bark-cloth). When fresh it relieved a variety of ailments including indigestion.

It is not surprising that Hawaiians enjoyed using *'awapuhi* for perfuming their homes, tapa and foods, as all members of the ginger family (originally from Asia) are renowned for their pleasant aroma or pungent spiciness. Cardamom seeds, for example, marvellous additions to cakes and curries, are of Indian origin.

'Awapuhi's fragrant leaves, usually less than three feet high, look a bit like wavy-edged *ti* leaves arranged alternately along an upright stalk. Here and there shorter stems arise, topped by conical flowerheads which exude copious quantities of the massage lubricant/shampoo described above. If you look closely at these flower heads, notice the tiny yellowish flowers poking out from behind the red-greenish

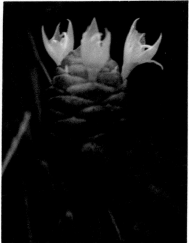

K. Kepler

Wild ginger blossoms.

J. Carothers

A ginger flower nestled among leaves.

overlapping, petal-like leaves. These rather strange flowers are the equivalents of the much larger, familiar, yellow ginger blossoms.

Wild ginger needs to be warm, wet and shaded. It prefers fairly open, darkish regions on windward sides of our islands where rainfall is plentiful. In places it forms an almost continuous ground cover. It often grows on abandoned taro terraces near Hawaiian village sites, often in company with *kukui*, breadfruit (*'ulu*) or mountain apple trees.

Noticeable along our windward highways are several species of Asian gingers: red, shell, yellow, white, torch and kahili. The showy, butterfly-shaped flowers of the last three possess an ethereal delicacy of form and an enchanting, romantic odor. Even their scientific name, *Hedychium*, "sweet snow", reflects these properties! They have been used for lei-making and garden beautification even since their introduction into Hawaii last century. It is thought that the Chinese brought them.

Attractive though they be, however, these tall gingers are a real nuisance in our native forests. After arrival they escaped from the confines of home gardens and crept rapidly along watercourses, choking out native ferns and tree seedlings, all the time spreading their thick, pink rhizomes and tenacious roots along the ground in every direction. Today in some wet lowland forests (for example, *mauka* of Hana, Maui and Alakai Swamp, Kauai) hundreds of acres of former forest are strangled by these naturalized ornamentals. Nothing can compete with their aggressiveness.

In this connection, any ginger is simple to propagate. Merely cut or break a length of rhizome ("root") with some true roots attached and plant it. The only trouble you'll have is controlling its growth. Keep your garden pick handy! Red gingers are even easier to grow, as their baby plants grow in an unusual fashion right out of the long, red, cylindrical flower clusters.

'Awapuhi lau pala wale ..... "It is a ginger leaf; it ripens quickly... mused the old Hawaiians in reference to anything that passed too soon. Wild ginger's luxuriant leaves, with their numerous leaflets, certainly yellow quite fast, but new ones are always sprouting too, reminding us of the continuation and transitory nature of Life.

Scientific Names: wild ginger (*Zingiber zerumbet*), edible ginger (*Z. officinale*), yellow ginger (*Hedychium flavescens*), white ginger (*H. coronarium*), kahili ginger (*H. gardnerianum*), torch ginger (*Phaeomeria magnifica*), red ginger (*Alpinia purpurata*).

Other names for wild ginger: 'awapuhi, 'awapuhi kuahiwi, shampoo ginger.

Family: Zingiberaceae or gingers, about 1400 species; related to all gingers, turmeric, cardamom.

K. Kepler

Yellow ginger, fragrant, attractive... and a nuisance.

Brilliant red ginger.

Torch ginger bud. Its pink "petals" are actually modified leaves.

K. Kepler

FALSE STAGHORN
FERN (uluhe)

Purple fiddleheads unfold wiry tissues.

Perspiring profusely, Sam Kalalau and his two companions, Mike and Talmedge, unbuckle the hipbelts on their heavy packs and collapse backwards onto a springy patch of *uluhe* ferns. *Uluhe!* For nearly two days they have been constantly hacking trail through it, and they have not yet reached their initial goal, a grassy knoll at the top of their present ridge. As they progressed from lowland pineapple fields, the *uluhe* changed from an ankle-high ground cover to nine vertical feet of solid, interlocking stems and stiff, comb-like fronds towering above their heads. At times their only recourse was to carve tunnels through it. Every time they slashed their machetes, dozens of needle-sharp stems scratched them. They needed to be constantly aware of their eyes, for a poke in the eye, they knew, was very painful and could cause permanent damage. It was imperative too, to be conscious of concealed logs; Sam had already hurt his knee on one.

To negotiate steep inclines, the young men needed to cling onto the *uluhe* with their left hands, hitch up their packs and slash with their right arms. Scramble, grab, slash, slip... whoops, scramble, grab, slash... again and again. Another section is completed.

Now they take a breather. Hawaii's introduced biting flies swarm and buzz round them, attracted to their sweat. Heat from a cloudless sky beats down on their heads and a swig of plastic tasting warm water tastes unbelievably refreshing.

Silently they share the desire never to see *uluhe* again, but instead of grumbling, they joke around and try to forget the hardships of their job (U.S. Fish and Wildlife Service forest surveys). By the time radio-check time rolls around they are in good spirits, raving about the magnificence of the surrounding scenery.

Ahead an awesome V-shaped valley plunges into the heart of West Maui's mountains. Sheer cliffs hundreds of feet high drop precipitously to the gurgling river below. Dozens of waterfalls tumble down the water-worn shutes, gathering momentum as they disappear into a sea of green blanketing the valley floor. It's a long way down there! They do not know it yet, but two more days' work ahead of them awaits Maui's most spectacular waterfall, a 1900' high gem that descends in two tiers at the head of the valley.

These boys are not the first hikers to encounter *uluhe*'s difficulties. To those who veer off Hawaii's established mountain trails, *uluhe* is a definite reality that provokes mixed emotions. While you may appreciate its attractiveness and value as a hardy colonizer of fresh mudslides and ridges, its compact thickets may be so frustrating and fatigueing that negative emotions quickly surface. Some people spill them out in a barrage of unmentionable language; other stoically endure it, the exhaustion on their faces bearing testimony to its enervating effects.

Uluhe, although often a formidable barrier, is not quite as impenetrable as a *hau* thicket. You *can* pass through it (if it's high enough you'll need a machete), although as you become entangled in its criss-cross, sharp-stemmed meshes you may wish you'd never tried. It can also provide a false sense of security. *Uluhe*'s masses can sustain you temporarily over narrow gullies, but musical tinkles of water far below spell peril. In 1979 another U.S. Fish and Wildlife Survice Survey member, Peter Payton, suddenly fell through a mat of *uluhe* into a deep hidden lava crack in the Big Island's Puna district. After ricocheting 130 feet down this jagged, narrow chasm, he finally landed on a ledge and managed to stabilize himself. Fortunately he survived, but not without multiple cuts and bruises, a few broken bones, and months of recuperation.

Four species of *uluhe* inhabit our islands, all found nowhere else in the world. The common one, with its apple-green, forked fronds (about one foot across), which divide successively in twos, is easy to identify either closely or at a distance. It covers slopes, ridges and roadcuts in the windward areas of our islands, mostly below 4000 feet.

Giant *uluhe,* growing deeper within forests, is so huge that its forked fronds may measure 11 feet across! The Hawaiians, appropriately, called it *"uluhe-lau-nui",* "the *uluhe* with big leaves".

New fiddleheads are gorgeous. From an underground creeping stem each uncurls from a tight circle, exposing a shiny stem, colored a stunning shade of purple. Each of these stalks seems to exude an "air of assurance", as though it will take over its little world. And each one does. Growing rapidly, spreading and creeping, each contributes to an entangled mass that piles up higher and higher. Beneath the living layers, dead fronds drop and decay, enriching the ground beneath, and acting as a nursery for seedling trees, shrubs and more ferns.

In 1933, C.S. Judd, an Oahu forester, decided to test whether *uluhe* effectively covered fresh landslides. He removed *uluhe* from an experimental patch of steep ground. Fresh ferns immediately began to invade it from the edges at a rate of *three to seven feet per year*! He was pleased that, as a result of this phenomenal rate of growth, his plot showed no signs of erosion, thanks to the heavy mat of fern debris. However, it might have been a fire hazard; occasionally foresters need to

A view worth uluhe's *hardships. Honokohau Valley, Maui.*

Cutting trail through a tough, matted uluhe *thicket.*

K. Kepler

Wildlife Service

K. Kepler

Common uluhe *entering a grassy roadcut.*

K. Kepler

Waterfalls streaming to a rushing torrent in the valley below, W. Maui.

fight fires on sunny ridges in othewise wet areas. The reason is that once a fire begins, the large amounts of brittle, dead material below the green ferns acts as additional fuel to feed the fire, which may sweep over many acres.

One fascinating creature lives beneath all this fern debris. Of course there are plenty beetles and other insects, but this one is very unusual. It is a damselfly, which looks like a small dragonfly. Forsaking the tradition of raising young in streams or pools, this particular species, unique to Hawaii, nurtures its nymphs in the moist earth under *uluhe* ferns. It has thus become modified to live and breathe in air, rather than to extract oxygen from flowing water.

Uluhe had few uses in old Hawaii. An infusion of its fronds served as an occasional bitter laxative. People did not use it for basketry, probably because it was too brittle. Nor did they thatch huts with it. On Oahu recently, however, other Polynesians have artfully created thick roofing with it. You can see one of these huts near the entrance of the Polynesian Cultural Center.

Uluhe seems to typify our paths of living. At times it is pretty to observe or easy to negotiate. At other times it creates an almsot insurmountable barrier; we can turn back or muster up extra energy and determination to pass through.

Scientific Names: common *uluhe, Dicranopteris linearis;* giant *uluhe, Hicriopteris pinnata.*
Other Names: uluhe, uluhi, comb-bracken, false staghorn fern
Family: Gleicheniaceae, chiefly a tropical fern family, about 150 species.

MAIDENHAIR

FERN

('iwa'iwa)

Dripping, humid, lowland valleys – favored haunts of maidenhair ferns.

The Hawaiian Islands are beautiful... no one needs to be told that. We all appreciate our islands in different ways. For those who are attracted to mountains and who aspire for adventure and grandiose scenery, the rewards are manifold.

The first foreign visitors to Maui admired its mountains from afar. As is true today, a very small percentage of them proceeded beyond the populated lowlands and lower hill slopes (already greatly altered by Hawaiians) to penetrate the rugged mountain ridges and valleys. Those who did applauded the beauty they encountered. Simultaneously they were overwhelmed by the dangerous, awe-inspiring nature of the terrain.

Unfortunately few of Hawaii's guests or residents, even up till now, were proficient in writing of their experiences. We had no John Muirs, Henry Thoreaus or Aldo Leopolds to describe the magnificent pristine glory of our native forests and luxuriant valleys, or to ponder on the philosophical questions that such scenery inspired.

Archibald Menzies was one of the better early writers. A Scottish botanist, he was surgeon and naturalist for Capt. George Vancouver in the years 1792-1794. In this capacity he was the first educated white man to organize an expedition into West Maui's mountains. He writes of how the forest was "difficult and dangerous to traverse from its ruggedness, hideous caverns and rocky precipices" and of how he was "embosomed in a woody, deep, narrow chasm with overhanging black precipices of immense height on both sides".

It is all true. Dripping from the declivitous rocky walls he must have seen thousands of maidenhair ferns, with their membranous, apple-green leaflets. Arising from thick vertical carpets of mosses, these lacy plants flowed gently downwards, brightening otherwise gloomy ravines with their delicate beauty (see inside covers). We also know that in these valleys Menzies was surrounded by tangles of numerous other species of water-loving ferns and plants, many of which are rare today.

A few years ago I gained some insight into how Menzies must have felt when he ventured into that steep, narrow valley behind Lahaina (probably Olowalu Valley).

Apple-green delicacy enhances rocky banks.

A British biologist was staying with us, and with a hiking background like Menzies, he was not quite prepared for Maui's surprises! I took him into a West Maui valley where maidenhair ferns blanket mossy rock faces hundreds of feet high. We waded, entranced, through a bouldery stream in an incredibly narrow gorge embowered by ferns, while a gentle shower-like curtain of water sprayed us. At the neck of the gorge, the ever-present water had channeled itself into a typically Hawaiian bouncing, unscalable waterfall. Menzies himself could not have been more entranced!

Maidenhairs love water and high humidity; they need it to grow luxuriantly. To see them in the wild, one generally needs to enter narrow gulches or shady streambeds where the sun rarely penetrates. Deep lowland valleys practically anywhere in windward areas (even along roadsides) should reward you with these pretty, hanging ferns. Their soft, almost transparent tissues, with tuning-fork-shaped veins, rarely tolerate drying-out. On the other hand, to prevent becoming waterlogged, they possess a waterproofing agent in their thin smooth leaves. This substance must have given rise to their scientific name, *Adiantum,* which means "unwettable". Think of maidenhairs as the plant equivalent of ducks, whose feathers resist matting together when wet.

Hawaii has five species of native maidenhairs, plus several introduced ones. None like high elevations. About 1000 feet is their upper elevational limit.

A maidenhair is one of the easiest types of ferns to identify. Its lacy, triangular leaves are divided twice to form many scalloped, fan-shaped leaflets. Their brown spore-clusters are moon-shaped and positioned along the underside margins of the leaves. Their fine, shiny leafstalks, resembling black enameled wire, are very brittle. Nevertheless, they were used on rare occasions by the old Hawaiians to weave designs on *lauhala* purses, or fashion delicate items such as baskets, fishtraps or other ornaments. In the Maui Historical Museum is a lovely ladies' hat woven entirely from these glossy, dark fern stems.

Maidenhairs have long been popular as house- or garden plants. They can be fussy, but if you try them, tend them gently by avoiding drafty places and excessive heat. Spray them often with a mister. The best soils are moist, rich and loose, full of fiber.

It is always a pleasure to encounter maidenhairs in their natural setting. Such delight stems not entirely from the ferns themselves, but from the whole experience of reaching their location and enjoying the beauty and tranquillity once you are there. You may have scratched legs, wet pants, muddy boots and messed-up hair, but who cares? You are priveleged to peek into a relatively untouched past that extends back hundreds of thousands of years.

Not everything comes to us easily. There will always be special places, both in nature and in our hearts, that require some degree of hardship or discipline to reach. And I think we will all agree that such secret spots are worthy of every ounce of effort expended!

Scientific Names: Adiantum species
Other names: 'iwa'iwa, maidenhairs, Venus-hair fern
Family: Polypodiaceae, the largest fern family.

SADLERIA

FERN

('ama'uma'u)

Sadleria ferns and cascades after heavy rains.

Hawaiian ladies carrying handwoven bags walk from all directions towards a meeting-place in Waimea, Oahu. It is "recycling day". Members of their large *'ohana* (extended family) have amassed many pieces of old worn tapa (bark-cloth) and are planning to weld the strips together. The production of new tapa is a lengthy, time-consuming process, and this family have for years utilized the native fern, *ama'uma'u,* to prolong the usefulness of used tapa.

Manufactured entirely from beating the soaked fibers of paper mulberry bark, tapa becomes thin and holey very quickly in Waimea's hot, perpetually moist climate. It cannot be washed or wrung out and literally falls apart as its fibers separate under stresses of daily activity.

Yesterday the people hiked into the deep mountain valleys to collect armfuls of *ama'uma'u* fronds. Several women now dislodge small chunks of a green pulpy paste from their stems. This is their glue. It is solid but mucilaginous. They place this adhesive onto the tapa scraps, then beat it in along the edges, joining them in quilt-like fashion. The beater, appropriately, is a rolled-up fern frond, adding more adhesive during the flailing process.

So recycling is not new after all! Actually, the effective utilization of materials and resources is a distinctive feature of islanders. Attention to the fundamentals of survival – fresh water, adequate food, shelter and clothing were, and still are, especially crucial on isolated islands. Hawaiians, particularly those living in areas where it took a great deal of effort to replace basic necessities, lived in part by the principles of "waste not, want not". Customs existed such as tapa recycling, fishing taboos, and religious restraints.

Such practices varied greatly within communities and from year to year though. Sometimes their conservation ethics were sensible; at other times these same people were unnecessarily unkind to their land.

Mulching with *ama'uma'u* fronds was one of the many areas where the old Hawaiians showed agricultural intelligence. Specializing in taro growing, they were

K. Kepler

C. Kepler

A hardy poineer in lava expanses.

A brilliant young frond.

able to produce it in both wet and dry areas. Before planting dryland taro they covered the fallow ground with fern fronds and other organic matter (*ti*, gingers etc.). When rain clouds approached they parted the mulch and planted taro seedlings, restoring the mulch after the rains to conserve water and hinder weeds. "Overhead the rain, clear away the mulch beneath" was a tidbit of wisdom from Hawaiian farmers.

If you imagine ferns as delicate, lacy plants embowering forested gullies and adding delicate beauty to dripping waterfalls, you are correct, but only partly! Ferns can be extremely hardy, especially in Hawaii where they may inhabit desolate areas where even grass and shrubs cannot grow. Our endemic (unique) *ama'uma'u* is probably one of the world's most rugged ferns!

It ranges from sea level to over 8000'; from coastal cliffs through deep shade in rain forests to windswept grasslands and bare lava flows in sub-alpine regions. It is easily recognized by its small trunk and stiffish fronds, three to four feet long (less lacy than the *hapu'u* treefern), and its young bronze-red leaves.

On the Big Island its habit of colonizing fresh lava flows is remarkable. Such ferns, dwarfed and leathery, may constitute the only plant life visible over vast stretches of *aa* lava.

Its most curious form may be seen in high elevation bogs, where mature, spore-producing *ama'uma'u* ferns may be as diminutive as a few inches high...they look like tiny color photos that have been lifted right out of a book and given life! Despite their hardiness and tolerance to a wide range of ecological conditions, *ama'uma'u* dies readily when transplanted from the wild to gardens. This is perhaps one reason why the old Hawaiians never cultivated it.

Being so widespread, this fern had other uses besides tapa recycling – temporary housing, famine food, dyes and weaving. Incidentally, overlapping dead fronds laid beneath a pup tent provide a delightfully spongy mattress which is both comfortable and sometimes a necessary protection against jagged lava or squishy mud.

An unusual view of Keanae Peninsula, Maui.

Birth, life and death coexist in this uniquely Hawaiian fern. Every *ama'uma'u* has many dead fronds that droop downwards, partly covering its trunk. Above these is a circular layer of living, arching, green fronds, while one or two pink-bronze fiddleheads unfold from its central growing point. Each fresh burst of life exhibits such a vibrancy and radiance that one's eyes cannot help but linger on the beauty. Fern fronds such as this have been emerging in rosy symmetry, living briefly, and dying for millions of years. Each in its prime is a classical example of perfection, yet how rapidly it is replaced by another of equal exquisiteness! How can any of us feel indispensible in this world if we contemplate such a natural flow of events?

Strong fiddlehead and mature leaves.

Names: *Ama'uma'u* or common sadleria (*Sadleria cyatheoides*)

Family: Blechnaceae, a worldwide fern family. Hawaii has seven species of sadlerias.

TREEFERN

(hapu'u)

K. Kepler

A fiddlehead fit for a symphony.

Filtered light streams through the forest canopy highlighting the understory verdure. As if by magic, all gloominess is dispelled and you are standing in a fairy-land. Embowering you in apple-green lucency are delicate, lacy treefern fronds, demanding your recognition of their exquisite color and symmetry. From the center of each stately treefern arise erect, furry stems, proudly crowned by woolly, unfurling spirals bearing a striking resemblance to the scrollheads of orchestral double basses. What archaic tunes can be heard from Nature's fiddles?

Let us listen. Dripping water plops sweet, glockenspiel-like ringing tones from arching fern fronds to a ground level pool; spore-cases from older fronds "pop" their sporecases in tiny explosions; and scurrying insect feet patter across the sparkling greenery. Avian choruses tinkle and twitter in the background, and treetrunks groan as the wind constantly tests their flexibility.... all are perfect accompanists to the whispering notes murmuring from hundreds of ferny fiddleheads ranging in size from smaller than the tiniest Suzuki violin, to larger than the extinct "great double basses". A symphony is there – we only need to attune ourselves to its music.

What would a rainforest be like without treeferns? Much less charming, as we know from comparison with those Hawaiian forests which have lost them. Flourish-ing over several thousand feet of elevation, Hawaii's six species of endemic treeferns require a steady and abundant supply of water. Given shade from larger trees they form (especially on the Big Island) an almost continuous secondary layer of forest greenery, in turn protecting more fragile ferns, vines and ground-loving plants. Gullies and narrow valleys, providing high humidity, are especially favored.

Hapu'u, as the old Hawaiians called them, instead of being true woody trees, act more like rosettes of ferns living atop their own dead stems. A single "trunk", which may attain 25 feet in height and 20 inches in diameter, is composed of only a central column of starch ensheathed in the bases of old fronds and intertwining aerial roots. There are no plant vessels to conduct water and sap from roots to fronds. As most gardeners in Hawaii know, one must water *hapu'u* at the top,

K. Kepler

A hapu'u *slope in undisturbed rain forest,*
Olokui, Molokai.

A healthy treefern in pig-free surroundings,
Olokui, Molokai.

where new fronds arise, rather than adjacent to the roots. (A note to gardeners: frequent watering and occasional doses of liquid fertilizer at the base of the fronds should keep your *hapu'u* healthy and green.)

All over the world, in both temperate and tropical regions, native peoples have utilized treeferns, both dead and alive. The Hawaiians were no exception, occasionally paving forest paths with them or eating them. The interlacing trunk fibers are today especially prized by orchid and anthurium growers who value a sterile substratum onto which aerial roots can attach.

As much as 70 lbs of pure starch may be laid down over the years in the treefern's central "core", a fair source of carbohydrate. In bygone days, whole trunks were freed of their outer fibers, cooked, then split to provide food for either people or pigs. Pigs do not require that starch be steamed; one of the tell-tale signs of a high feral pig population in our rainforests today is the presence of gauged-out *hapu'u* trunks, sad reminders of a formerly pristine condition.

Around 1920 a starch industry was begun on the Big Island, producing *hapu'u* starch to be used for cooking and laundry. Threatening large tracts of beautiful forest, this industry was fortunately halted after a short time.

Undoubtedly the most useful of *hapu'u's* gifts to the old Hawaiians was a rather unusual, soft flocculent product called *pulu*. This silky fluff, gathered in handfuls from unfolding fiddleheads, is composed of thousands of golden-brown scales which protect the young buds and stembases of the plant. Under normal circumstances, little of this was taken; its chief use was for embalming the dead, an interesting process. After the corpse was eviscerated, it was stuffed with *pulu,* sewed up with *oloná* cord, wrapped in black tapa for several months, then finally buried. It has recently been found that *pulu* contains an acid which absorbs body liquids and dries up a deceased human body so that its skin feels like parchment, hence lengthening its "life".

After white man arrived, *pulu's* potential was realized and village chiefs were more than ready to order their villagers into the forest to collect it by sackfuls to be sold overseas. Orders were to collect everything, even to cutting down a treefern if it was too high, in order to reach its few meagre handfuls of *pulu.* Between 1867 and 1884 an astonishing amount of sun-dried *pulu* was exported – over four million pounds! It padded everything stuffable: pillows, mattresses, quilts, dead bodies and toys. It raised much money for a nation now exposed to the materialistic world and suffering from debts left from the Sandalwood Era.

Although at first glance an acceptable substitute for down – light, airy and soft, *pulu* unfortunately was found to provide only temporary comfort. Judd, an early Hawaiian forester, commented in 1927 on *pulu* pillows: "When new, these were admirable, but after the thread-like cells had broken down the mattresses became lumpy and an old *pulu* pillow was just as comfortable as a bag of very fine sand."

Today, with the exception of regulated *hapu'u* cutting for landscaping, and the occasional fronds lopped off for cooking, Hawaii's treeferns are not endangered by man's activities. Perhaps *hapu'u's* most practical use is to provide a snuggly lining for bird's nests, certainly no drain on the ecosystem and a small comfort provided to several species of birds who glean insects from its arching fronds.

If you are fortunate to find yourself in a lovely rainforest such as Hawaii Volcanoes National Park, take a brief walk. Don't worry if it's wet. Attune your eyes to fine details of color and texture within this sylvan setting. Listen for the subtle symphony of natural sounds ringing clear within the crystalline air. And feel that palpable vibrancy which uplifts your spirit.

Scientific Names: Cibotium spp *(glaucum, hawaiense, menziesii, nealiae, st. johnii)*
Family: Dicksoniaceae, a treefern family mostly represented in the southern hemisphere; about 40 species.

Plenty of pulu *protects the stems of this Kauai treefern.*

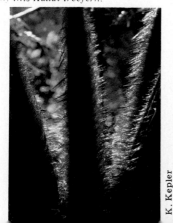

K. Kepler

Treeferns add an extra dimension to Hawaii's mountain scenery.

C. Kepler

HALA

What coastal scene is not embellished by hala? *Hoalua Bay, Maui.*

Regarded as a nature spirit (*kupua*) in ancient Hawaii, the picturesque *hala* or pandanus tree has been revered, utilized and loved for centuries by Pacific people. Every portion of the growing and mature plant provided materials for housing, food, medicine, ornaments, fishing implements, religion and folklore.

According to Hawaiian tradition, this very tree contributed to the origin of mankind: a beautiful young goddess was once busy cutting *hala* strips for mat-weaving, when her shell-trimmer slipped and cut her finger. The finger bled profusely, and as the blood coagulated, two eggs formed. From these eggs emerged the mother and father of the human race.

Science and folklore often meet on common ground; ideas expressed in ancient chants or tales may have a scientific basis. In this case, the idea of *hala* being so old that it relates to our origin bears truth in the fact that pandanus trees are some of the world's oldest known plants, dating back over 250 million years.

In old Hawaii, this tree, with its short trunk bearing forked branches topped by attractive, spiral tufts of leaves, was abundant in moist lowlands. Some groves were sacred, such as those at Hanalei and Haena (Kauai), Kahala and Nuuanu (Oahu), Puna (Big Is.) and the Waianapanapa-Hana area (Maui).

The *hala's* trunk bears multiple aerial roots as it grows, which extend downwards as props, supporting an ever-increasing weight of branches and leaves. Our most common one, the female tree, bears pineapple-like fruits. These multiple-fruited balls mature from green to orange or red, then drop their numerous colorful fleshy fruitlets to the ground.

While outwardly almost identical to the female, the male tree is composed of

A coastal hala *thicket towers above beach naupaka.*

A pile of fallen hala *seedpods, potential "paintbrushes".*

...though in a rugged setting, hala *is always ...se to the coast.*

Hala's *aerial "prop" roots, ancient medicine.*

much harder wood.   Its drooping flower-clusters, composed of hundreds of pale flowers (the famous *hinano* in Hawaiian song and poetry) liberate masses of extremely fragrant pollen.

These flower-clusters were gathered in former times by local maidens to lure youths of their particular fancy.   They either chased the young men with dangling clusters, sprinkling the pollen over their bodies in a playful manner, or collected the pollen for more subtle uses such as aphrodisiacs (perfumed oils and tapas).

The spiny *hala* leaves (*lauhala*) were used extensively as floor-coverings in the old days.   *Hala's* natural, lustrous "plastic" finish is impervious to dirt, food and may be water-repellent.   Today an old Hawaiian mat is a prized possession or museum-piece.

By the time an Hawaiian girl was a teenager, she knew two dozen-odd names for the different parts of the *hala* plant, could recognize six basic leaf-types and could weave small, coarse mats using strips ½ to 1 inch wide.   Her mother and grandmother, with many years of experience, deftly produced larger mats of at least 20 different shapes, sizes and grades.   The finest ones utilized thread-like strips up to 16 per inch!

Today in many Pacific islands the chief occupation of older women is still that of weaving *lauhala* mats – whether they call them *hala, fala, ha'a* or *hara,* the finished product is still the same.   Making mats is very time-consuming, involving cutting, drying, de-spining, rolling, beating, dyeing (if necessary) and finally weaving.

Hawaiians also braided *hala* canoe sails, sandals, rectangular pillows, fans and baskets.   They knew how to concoct medicines too, primarily from the tips of growing shoots and aerial roots.   These parts of the *hala* plant are equivalent to our highly nutritious and vitamin loaded bean sprouts... it is not surprising that they contained healing power!

The fruitlets ("keys") were also useful.   Used as leis, their symbolism varied: at New Year such a lei symbolized good luck, and during the rest of the year, bad luck.

The dry fruitlets, ideal protective jackets for several tiny seeds, resemble stubby

C. Kepler

Hala *leaves almost ready to weave, Savaii, Western Samoa.*

K. Kepler

Most South Pacific ladies still weave regularly. Ofu, American Samoa.

paintbrushes. These were formerly important in staining and varnishing *tapa* (bark-cloth). Even today children like to collect them for use in artwork. Look for them on lawns, sand, gardens and parking lots: in short, wherever you see *hala* growing.

Long ago the *hala* signified seasons for people living in calendarless times. When *hala* fruits ripened, Hawaiian fishermen grabbed their *uhu* (parrotfish) lines and headed for the reefs, their wives carried baskets to the shallow waters to gather *wana* (sea-urchins), and the less energetic strung leis from *hala's* colorful fruitlets.

Wending their way across thousands of miles of trackless ocean, *hala* seeds (originally from Malaysia) arrived in Hawaii via natural and Polynesian means, becoming a native tree which provided many basics for human survival on our remote archipelago.

> *"The voice of Puna's sea resounds*
> *Through the echoing hala groves. . .*
> *The leaves of the twisted hala,*
> *The sheath of its perfumy bloom –*
> *All torn by the rage of the storm."*

from an ancient Hawaiian chant

Scientific Name: Pandanus odoratissimus
Other names: hala, puhala, pandanus, screwpine
Family: Pandanaceae or Screwpine family; about 156 species; related to true palms.

HAU

Hau *blossom: ancient symbol of the human spirit.*

Two active young Hawaiian boys race down a well-worn track towards Paia, Maui. Occasionally they leap into the air or punch one another playfully. Their father follows behind carrying net bags and woven baskets. He has just obtained permission from his village chief to collect branches from the *hau* tree, a much-esteemed plant with heart-shaped leaves that grows particularly well on Maui's windward coast.

Upon arriving at the shore, all three dive, porpoise-fashion, into the cool waves, body-surfing back to shore a few times as they enjoy the refreshing water. Their father notices that someone has placed *hau* branches all along the shoreline above high-tide mark. He explains to his children that this is the chief's *kapu* (taboo). No-one is allowed to fish in these shallow waters until the *hau* is removed. Violation is punishable by death. All the village men realize that many types of baby fish need inshore nursery-grounds at this time of year, and that they should not be bothered while they are maturing. After this crucial period in the sheltered shallows, most will swim into or beyond the reefs to complete their development.

The family walks along the beach to a dense *hau* thicket. Branches intertwine and criss-cross, forming an almost impenetrable jungle.

Eagerly the boys help to chop off many of the light and pliable branches with their crude adzes, carved years ago from *hau* wood and volcanic stone. Their inner cores will be perfect for fishing net floats. *Hau's* corky wood is so light that these little floats will retain their bouyancy for years (in fact, Christmas Islanders still prefer them to plastic floats). From the outer bark that is stripped off, village men will fashion shark nooses, sandals and heavy, prickly ropes.

As the sun glows pink behind West Maui's mountains, the family slowly trudges back up Haleakala's slopes, laden with bundles of bark-strips, branches and cuttings. The smallest lad tucks a tiny piece of wood into his *malo* (loincloth) for his grandfather to carve into a toy canoe. A light outrigger craft, lashed together with *hau* and coconut fibers, caulked with breadfruit gum and fitted with a sail of braided

An impenetrable tangle of hau *branches.*

K. Kepler

Ephemeral beauty prepares for disintegration in the leaf litter.

hala leaves.... he can already envision it sailing on a little pool in the gulch near his hut.

Hau, a tree, or more correctly a high hedge, is a type of hibiscus. It grows on all of Hawaii's inhabited islands from sealevel up to approximately 2000'. Widely-distributed throughout the Pacific and other tropical regions, it is apparently not native to Hawaii, even though its buoyant seeds can germinate after months in sea-water. Anthropologists believe that cuttings and seeds were carried here in the earliest canoes from more southern islands, together with breadfruit, taro, sweet potatoes and other food and medicinal plants.

Still planted on Maui today, *hau* makes a wonderful windbreak and helps stabilize coastal soils. To grow it you merely insert cuttings into the soil and keep them wet.

Although not loudly proclaimed, a few obscure references indicate that to some it was sacred, its legendary genealogy leading directly back to the great gods of Polynesia. Even more importantly, man's precious spark of life, his soul, has been likened to the *hau's* ephemeral flower, which unfurls yellow in the morning, turns orange in the afternoon, then withers and dies a dark orange by nightfall.

Hau may be observed in many localities in Hawaii, primarily in wettish coastal areas along the north shores of all the major islands, even in settled regions. Its masses of tangly branches, profusion of heart-shaped leaves and scattered, gay yellow blossoms are unmistakeable.

In associating *hau* blossoms, which exhibit their delicate beauty only a few hours, with the human spirit, the Hawaiians must have understood much about the transitory nature of Life. Springing from the wellspring of Life, the great Polynesian gods, this strong spreading tree constantly buds forth beautiful, fresh blossoms, symbols of human souls .... perhaps this allows us today to respect more the spiritual understandings of old Hawaii and to reflect anew on the ephemerality of man.

A pregnant lady strolls along the rocky shoreline at Kaena Point with her three small children. She halts periodically to pluck fresh *limu* (seaweed) and *pupu* (black sea-snails); these she pops into her coarse net bag made from *hau* fibers. As the family slowly works its way around the peninsula they are pleased that their home-woven sandals (also made from *hau* bark) protect their feet so well from the jagged lava rocks.

Approaching a thick stand of *hau,* the lady picks a few flowerbuds and hands them to her toddler who need her innards flushed out a bit (too much poi!). She wonders about her fourth baby as she drips some sticky *hau* sap into her gourd. The midwife will smear this onto her vagina to lessen pain during childbirth, simultaneously lubricating her newborn's passage into the world. She will also mix this sap with grated coconut for a shampoo and hair-cleanser. Her oldest daughter strips off a few pieces of *hau* bark on which to thread some shells for a lei.

This imaginary scene was not necessarily restricted to Kaena or Oahu, or even the Hawaiian Islands. *Hau,* a coastal hibiscus tree, is dispersed throughout the Pacific and has been used extensively for centuries by her oceanic peoples. That it was carried, or occurred naturally, practically everywhere is reflected in the similar names used in widely-separated island groups: *hau, fau, vau, fou* and *purau.*

One of its traditional uses was in generating fire. Before matches arrived in Hawaii, fire was produced by rubbing a slender, pointed hardwood stick back and forth in a groove in a larger piece of soft *hau* wood. The sparks were rapidly transferred to a piece of tapa (bark-cloth), blown on, then used to kindle a larger flame elsewhere.

Rolls of hau *fibres amidst local produce, Apia Market, Western Samoa.*

Hau was such an outstandingly useful plant in Pacific cultures (akin to other botanical necessities such as coconut, *hala* and *kukui*), that it is mind-boggling to enumerate its uses. It provided materials for medicines, canoes, cordage, clothing, weapons such as slings, houses, tools such as adzes, fishing gear, games such as kites, strainers, rituals and even spectacular fireworks displays.

Hau and *oloná* (a type of nettle) provided the bulk of fibrous materials used in ancient Hawaii. In our archipelago, however, fibers made from *hau's* coarse outer bark was used more frequently than fibers from its whiter, finer inner bark which were used almost exclusively in the rest of the Pacific. In Tahiti, for instance, women beat these fine fibers into bark-cloth, split it finely, or wove it into intricate, linen-like materials and exquisite matting. Next time you watch traditional Tahitian dancing, examine closely the girls' swishy "grass" skirts –if they are authentic they will be made from finely-split *hau* bark.

Most people in Hawaii today would not know that to do with *hau,* but not so for our contemporary "neighbors". Walk into the open market in Apia, Western Samoa, and you will see bundles of fine *hau* fibers offered for 20¢ each by local vendors. What, you might inquire, are they for? Early Sunday mornings, in every village, every family will use them in the preparation of their main weekly hot meal. Father hand-grates some coconuts, then mother squeezes the gratings through the *hau* fibers into a large bowl. With strong wrist movements she wrings and wrests the hard coconut meat through the wiry fibers. Quarts of remarkably rich coconut cream streams into the bowl. This cream is subsequently mixed with taro tops and onions (or fish), wrapped in leaves and steamed underground for several hours to create *palusami,* a sumptuous (and terribly filling!) dish.

Old and new: hau *fishing floats on nylon netting. Christmas Is., Central Pacific.*

Hau even made its debut out of island cultures into the world of commerce in the form of English cricket bats. Quite a business was established in Jamaica to this end. Its combination of strength and lightness was ideal.

During the early 19th Century, when Tahiti's people were suffering greatly from many of white man's scourges, priests became very pessimistic. So many people died that priests announced the destruction of their nation. It could just as well have applied to Hawaii, where the same conditions existed. Annihilation of society was considered the greatest punishment that their gods could inflict upon them. The following was one of their predictions: "The *hau* shall grow, the branching coral shall spread out its branches, but man shall cease." In other words, *hau,* a fast-growing hardy tree, could continue to live under adversity; coral, covering vast areas of reef, would also survive, But man, a weaker living thing, would pass.

Our islands have seen many changes, some for better, some for worse. Yet *hau* lives on, still thriving along our coasts and wherever it is planted. It is a tough, resilient species.

Let us watch it carefully, for when it too disappears, a large portion of our Polynesian experience will truly be gone forever.

Hau *is usually close to both stream ocean and village.*

Scientific Name: Hibiscus tileaceus
Family: Hibiscus family or Malvaceae; about 1500 species; related to *milo, 'ilima.*

Sling.

Hau *bark Sandals.*

RED

HIBISCUS

(kokio 'ula)

R. Hobdy

*Hawaii's official State flower (*Hibiscus kokio*), rare in the wild.*

In 1923 an attractive red, silky-petalled hibiscus was designated as Hawaii's official flower. This emblem was not, as most believe, the common red Chinese hibiscus that grows ubiquitously in gardens and along roadsides. It was a native species called *koki'o - 'ula* (literally "red hibiscus"), once common on Oahu, Molokai and Maui, but now reduced to extreme rarity.

This particular hibiscus, which comes in several varieties, is a long-branched shrub that can reach 40' high under favorable conditions, although it is generally much smaller and less luxuriant than its introduced counterpart. Its blossoms vary in size and shape as well as color, ranging from pink to orange-red.

An interest in hibiscus was sparked in the 19th Century when Governor Archibald Cleghorn accomplished the first successful hibiscus hybridization. The potential for attractive ornamentals of multitudinous shapes, sizes and colors seemed enormous, and growing fascination with these lovely new hybrids mushroomed, not only in Hawaii, but throughout tropical and subtropical regions, including Southern California. Horticulturalists striving to secure desirable varieties introduced hibiscus into Hawaii from all over the world, culminating in the existence of over 5000 hybrids. Whole societies were, and still are, dedicated solely to their propagation.

By 1885 most of Hawaii's 33 species of native hibiscus were rare, having succumbed to the ravages of cattle and blight. Although amateur hybridizers utilized the red-flowered ones only infrequently for breeding experiments (the white ones were more popular), there was enough concern for their survival that many cuttings were brought into cultivation and attention was focussed on them by later declaring the *koki'o-'ula* Hawaii's official floral emblem. More recently, through the enthusiasm of State foresters, private citizens and organizations such as Outdoor Circle, the *koki'o-'ula,* although practically extinct in the wild, adorns streets, gardens and parks in a number of locations throughout our islands, and steps have been taken to preserve their remaining natural haunts. (By the way, if you own one, treat it as any hibiscus bush, watering well and pruning periodically to stimulate fresh flowering branches. Hibiscus, like fuschias, bloom most profusely on new growth. They also root readily from cuttings.)

Before cattle were introduced into Hawaii to roam freely over our lands, red hibiscus must have been readily available to Hawaiians both in wet and dry regions. They were used for decoration, rituals, tapa cloth, dyes and medicines. All parts of

Koki'o 'ula *in a very rare natural setting, Iao Valley, Maui.*

the plant are edible. Roots, flowerbuds, sap and leaves provided tonics to purify exhausted or clogged-up innards. For example, adults chewed buds and leaves to relieve constipation and even small doses of the mildly-acting buds were administered to babies. A traditional blood purifier incorporated red hibiscus roots pounded with dried treefern trunks and morning glory roots. Sugar cane was added to mask the taste of an otherwise unpalatable mixture. Many of us, who were required to swallow horrid medicines when we were children, can sympathize with the old Hawaiians who, according to recipes in old herbals, must have often tortured their taste-buds.

A few years ago an Hawaiian-Chinese lady asked me if she could pick some hibiscus buds from our garden to help cure a relative's boil. Even though the particular plant was introduced, she was carrying on a tradition that embraced all our native red hibiscus. She chopped unopened buds, combined them with Hawaiian salt and placed the mixture directly on the boil, covering it with cloth and tape. This poultice was changed every four days and eventually the boil burst, relieving the patient's painful pressure.

Hawaiians in bygone days also extracted a dark purple dye from the petals of red hibiscus flowers, as did the Chinese from their native species. For those of you familiar with Celestial Seasoning's "Red Zinger" tea, you may recall that its pink coloration is derived from red hibiscus petals. It is easy to concoct your own tea blends, using, for example, red hibiscus flowers, lemon grass and peppermint leaves. If you are serious about dyeing, Val Krohn, in "Hawaii Dye Plants and Dye Recipes" gives instructions for coloring wools with red hibiscus (any species will do). In this connection, do remember that although hibiscus flowers can last a day without water, their leis wilt rapidly and can easily stain the clothing of both lei giver and recipient if you extend your welcoming hug too long!

Synonymous with tropical glory and entrancing maidens, hibiscus flowers have lured untold millions to our fair islands. Unquestionably all hibiscus flowers are gorgeous, especially the ornamentals resulting from crossing the best varieties from all over the world. Hawaii's own hibiscus are also beautiful, and are special to us because they evolved here and are found nowhere else. I hope you have a chance to enjoy and appreciate them for their uniqueness and rarity. It is sad that our State Flower poises on the brink of extinction in the wild, and that most residents have never heard of it. I think you will agree, however, that it is a worthy part of our

Another native hibiscus, 'akiohala *(*Hibiscus Youngianus*)*

K. Kepler

Ma'o hau-hele *(*Hibiscus Brackenridgei*), a striking native Hawaiian hibiscus.*

K. Kepler

botanical heritage.

Scientific Name: Hibiscus kokio. The common red or Chinese hibiscus is a hybrid, *Hibiscus rosa-sinensis* X *schizopetale*
Other Names: native red hibiscus, *koki'o-'ula, koki'o-'ula'ula, pualoalo*
Family: Hibiscus or Malvaceae; about 1500 species; related to *'ilima, hau,* cotton.

K. Kepler

Hawaii's native cotton. Note the small, not-too-fuzzy seedpods and hibiscus – like flower.

WHITE

HIBISCUS

(koki'o ke'oke'o)

K. Kepler

Brilliant, fragrant blossoms: raw material for hybrids.

Colors in the tropical Pacific are dazzling. Bright and beautiful plants, ultramarine seas, gaudy reef fish, blazing sunsets – all have fascinated writers, artists and travelers for centuries.

Most of Hawaii's roadside and garden color, however, is imported from other countries; more species of plants have been introduced into Hawaii than to any other place on earth!

Even though the brilliance of many plants in continental tropical regions such as South-East Asia or Central America surpasses that of native vegetation on isolated Pacific islands, a few of Hawaii's own plants possess appreciable charm and flamboyance. They compare favorably with the prettiest plants in nurseries.

Our showy native white hibiscus (*koki'o ke'oke'o*) belong in this category. Attaining about 30 feet in height, I think these three species of trees, with their oval leaves and spectacular white flowers (about five inches in diameter) are Hawaii's most beautiful native flowering trees.

My favorite is the white Kauai hibiscus. Endemic (unique) to Kauai, it is found in a few localized valleys between 2000 and 3000 feet elevation in the Waimea Canyon area. In its natural surroundings, the huge, brilliant-white blossoms ("white-white" in Hawaiian) and long red central columns are conspicuous from afar. They splash large dots of color within the green verdure of sunny, luxuriant gullies, and their exquisite mellow fragrance (rare in the hibiscus family) pervades the rich humid air.

The Oahu species is similarly restricted to a few gullies within wet forests (such as Tantalus), and the Molokai one is so rare that only one location is currently known – in an isolated valley on the island's rugged north coast.

White hibiscus grow well in cultivation. Around 1900 the Kauai species was recognized as a plant worthy of world-wide recognition. Seeds were sent to other tropical regions such as Florida and the West Indies, where it now brightens gardens as an "exotic, introduced" hibiscus! The tables are turned as Hawaii, normally a recipient for foreign flowering plants, exports one of *her* natives.

Hawaii's white hibiscus also have a century-old history of hybridization. In this way they have contributed their genetic material to a plethora of beautiful horticultural hybrids. They number among our few native plants that have become successful economically, albeit it in a minor way.

Natural hybrids also occur when insects or native birds cross-pollinate native hibiscus with introduced varieties (such as the common red

Koaie Canyon, Kauai harbors a few of these rare shrubs.

Chinese hibiscus) that have become established along forest edges. Occasionally botanists encounter an unfamiliar wild hibiscus whose parentage and identification is a puzzle. Is it native or not? Is it a new species of just another mixed-up hybrid?

Unfortunately the pure species of Hawaiian white hibiscus are all restricted to small pockets of forests and are becoming rarer as years progress. It is only through the far-sightedness and concern of a few people who predicted their plights, that they have been saved from extinction. You can see some of these lovely rare species at botanical gardens such as Lyon and Waimea Arboretae (Oahu), Maui Botanical Garden, and Pacific Tropical Botanical Garden (Kauai).

In old Hawaii, white hibiscus were used primarily for decoration. People planted the shrubs close to their thatched huts and picked their flowers for ornament, much as we do with ornamental hibiscus today.

As we all know too well, early explorers, whalers and visiting haoles took delight in Hawaii's young, nubile girls – for many reasons. Not only did the men greatly enjoy the feminine favors of these dark-skinned damsels, they also loved their "natural jewelry": leis, head circlets and other hair decorations, all of native flowers and leaves. A late 18th Century drawing of an Hawaiian girl I once saw depicted a scantily-clad maiden with a large native white hibiscus in her long dark tresses. If my memory serves me correcly, the flower was over her *right* ear too ... who knows how the artist was paid for his portrait?!

Even though white hibiscus flowers, like many of our familiar colored hibiscus, will last a full day without drooping, they were not used for lei-making. The blossoms crushed and bruised too easily. Whenever fragrant white blossoms were desired for leis, ladies strung native gardenias into garlands.

Mentioned occasionally in ancient song and legend, Hawaii's native white hibiscus are truly floral treasures, worthy of all protection.

Scientific Names: White Kauai hibiscus, *Hibiscus waimeae*
Family: Malvaceae or hibiscus family; about 1500 species; related to *hau*, hollyhock.

'IE'IE

'Ie'ie: *orange spikes amidst* hala-*type leaves.*

Hundreds of years ago, in cultures all over the world, it was not unusual for people to believe that animals and plants could change into humans or vice versa. Polynesian mythology is laced with such tales: a man turns into a turtle, an eel into a coconut palm or a crab bears human babies. Naturally a god or goddess was always on hand to catalyse these remarkable transformations.

An Hawaiian legend concerning the origin of our endemic *'ie'ie* vine is of this nature; it concerns a beautiful maiden named Lau-ka-'ie'ie ("leaf of the 'ie'ie"). While still a baby, the Goddess Hina presented her to childless couple. She was raised with much love and care, developing into a charming, kind girl. She spent much time in the rainforest, where she became intimate with the native birds and flowers. Eventually she married a young man who also had a special affinity for birds, but soon it became time for her to change her form. Her eyes began to flash fiery, leaves sprouted all over her body, and she grew much taller and exceedingly slender. One day her husband advised her: "You do not need to be alone. Reach with your branches towards the sun and sky and climb the trees! Twine and grow around the trees with your long leaves! Your blazing red flowers shall shine between the leaves like fire. Give your beauty to all the *'ohi'a* trees in the forest!"

In this manner, Lau-ka-'ie'ie became the *'ie'ie* vine, always remaining close to her beloved forest friends. If I may take the liberty to add a contemporary biological touch, we see that as time progressed, birds such as the native *o'u* liked her presence so much that they came to depend primarily on her orange fleshy fruits for their livelihood. A number of uniquely Hawaiian insects also enjoyed her leaves as hiding places, and some even took up residence within her protective folds, refusing to move anywhere else (see photo, page 63)!

This latter comment deserves slight elaboration. Hawaii is renowned for its impressive lists of unusual plants and animals not found anywhere else in the world. Among them are forest shrimps (amphipods), wingless crickets and a leaf-hopper nymph, all of which have become so adapted to living in the leaf-axils of *'ie'ie* that they are flattened so as to fit between the leaf-bases. They live nowhere else. Here also, where water and organic debris collect, are two remarkable species of damselfly (like a small dragonfly) larvae. Instead of inhabiting streams, a damselfly's normal habitat, they have chosen to live in mini-ponds in the *'ie'ie,* way up in the trees.

'Ie'ie lends a tropical luxuriance to Hawaii's wet forests that cannot be matched

by any other native plant. (The large-leaved philodenrons that you see, say in Oahu's mountains and valleys, Maui's Hana Highway and the Big Island's Akaka Falls, are from South America.) Its woody, cylindrical stems twine gracefully around trees, sending out numerous tufts of narrow leaves, and an extensive network of aerial roots which clasp anything they contact. In season, from the center of certain bunches of leaves, emerge several orange-pink leaves and flowering spikes. Both leaves and spikes are reminiscent of pandanus (*hala*) a close relative.

I believe that *'ie'ie* has evolved very simply from *hala*. In lowland Samoa you can walk through dense *hala* forests where the trees are competing so strongly for light that their branches have become elongated, twining upwards around one another. It is like looking at a "missing link" between the regular *hala* tree and the *'ie'ie* vine. It is not too surprising that a plant might lean on another for support because as its branches lean upwards for light it becomes weaker and spindlier. If you keep your eyes open you can occasionally spot places in Hawaii where *hala* and *'ie'ie* grow together, resembling one another in form, although *hala's* leaves are larger.

To be a forest climber, having a slender stem supporting a large number of leaves (sometimes in a canopy over 60 feet high), a plant needs special adaptations. Such vines remind me of giraffes. Just as this long-necked mammal has many strong blood vessels equipped with valves to prevent blood from flowing backwards, so does the *'ie'ie* possess many long, rigid tubes for transferring its sap upwards against gravity's pull. Inside the stem these tubes are arranged like tight bunches of spaghetti, a typical pattern for woody vines.

Every inch or so, *'ie'ie's* sturdy stems are ringed with thickened bands of tissues, scars from old fallen leaves. These reinforce the long tubes just as tracheal rings reinforce our own windpipes. Where the vine flourishes best, curtains of entangling, intertwining, looping stems almost as impenetrable as a *hau* thicket may reach 40 to 50 feet in diameter. It is here that great tensile strength, flexibility and strong conducting tissues are imperative.

'Ie'ie is essentially a mountain plant in Hawaii today. It is found primarily from 1000 to 4000 feet elevation in wet, humid forests in windward areas. However, in former days it descended to sea level, adding a "jungly" character to the lavish variety of other vines, shrubs, trees and ferns that comprised our lush lowland forests. Isabella Bird Bishop, a 19th Century adventurer, writes (in 1875) of the rich forests around Hilo, Hawaii. Here were palms, *'ohi'a, koa, kukui,* papayas, treeferns and bamboos in abundance: "The lianas (vines) were there in profusion, climbing over the highest trees, and entangling them, with stems varying in size from those as thick as a man's arm to those as slender in size as whipcord, binding all in an impassable network, and hanging over our heads in rich festoons or tendrils swaying in the breeze. There were trailers (*'ie'ie*), with heavy knotted stems, as thick as a frigate's hawser, coiling up to the tops of tall *'ohi'a* with tufted leaves like yuccas, and crimson spikes of gaudy blossom. The shining festoons of the yam and the graceful trailers of the *maile*.... and glossy leaved climbers hung from tree to tree, and to brighten all, great morning glories of a heavenly blue opened a thousand blossoms to the sun, and gave a tenderer loveliness to the forest."

What a description! Very few lowland forests compare with that today, but *'ie'ie* vines still twine gracefully around thousands of tree-trunks on all our major islands where rainfall is high, and scramble along ridges where no trees are available. Finding one bearing a blaze of flower spikes (see title page) and surrounding leaves (Lau-ka-'ie-'ie's flaming eyes) is well worth any effort you might expend, although

A thicket of entangling 'ie'ie stems.

C. Kepler

unfortunately many are destroyed by tree-climbing rats, introduced forest vermin.

'Ie'ie was a sacred plant in old Hawaii. Dedicated to the forest god Ku, it formed a link with land and sea, with earth and sky, and with natural and supernatural. Perhaps it is not too silly to believe that a beautiful maiden can be transformed into a beautiful plant. After all, is not all life interconnected?

"It is the rain; thatch the house with 'ie'ie *vine for the fisherman's comfort,*
Thatch it again with the 'ie'ie *vine.*
'Ie'ie *baskets are the gatherers of the* nehu *fishers of Waiakea,*
In the rain, in the cold one is discouraged thereby."

from an old Hawaiian song

Reflections of an apricot dawn shimmer on the calm waters of Hanalei, Kauai. Three fisherman are loading circular woven traps into a canoe together with the rest of their fishing gear. Packets of bait, baked sweet potatoes wrapped in *ti* leaves, and extra stones to weight down the traps, are the last items to be included. For eight days the men have been baiting *'ie'ie* fishing baskets at selected sites in the reef, and today is the first day they will have a chance to capture some of their semi-tamed fish.

They first baited and lowered open baskets to the sea-floor, examining them for tooth marks at the end of four days. Large nibbles indicated that parrotfish (*uhu*) were nipping at their bait. Satisfied that there were plenty of fish, they next lowered another type of feeding basket, a little less open yet still without a funnel-shaped opening. This feeding continued for some days until the fish became accostomed to staying in these semi-enclosed baskets. Now it is time to lower the *'ie'ie* traps with internals funels; once having entered the *uhu* will not be able to exit.

As the men paddle their canoe out beyond the bay to the surge channels, where they hope to capture many of these gaudy blue, green and pink fish, they offer prayers to their fishing gods. Their age-old method works! No sooner have they lowered their traps than a gorgeous three-foot male finds himself ensnared. He thrashes around, banging against the sides of the trap, and slashes furiously as he is hauled into the boat. What an ideal offering to the gods! As the day progresses, the men catch dozens of *uhu* and their entire village celebrates when they return.

The wicker-like basketry of the Hawaiians, using long aerial rootlets from the *'ie'ie* vine, may be compared to the cane-basketry of many cultures. As similar vines to *'ie'ie* abound on all forested South Pacific Islands west of Hawaii all the way to Asia, it was natural for Hawaiians to use *'ie'ie* for baskets and fish-traps, just as their ancestors did.

In lush lowland forests, the *'ie'ie* climbs into the canopy, and it is here, rather than in the higher mountains, that their aerial rootlets grow longest. These rootlets differ from regular roots in that they are not buried in the ground. As the *'ie'ie*'s stem twirls around trunks and branches, it sends out hundreds of small roots to support itself, enabling it to advance even higher. Highly sensitive to touch, these rootlet tips cling to an object as soon as they touch it. But not all find a substrate, and some rootlets just keep growing. At canopy level, where the vine loops and droops down, some of these rootlets may hang down as much as ten feet in mid-air. Such long strands must have delighted the weavers of large fish-traps.

When the rootlets turned light brown, and their outer skin fell away when rolled between one's hands, they were ready for harvest. After storage in a dry place they were soaked in salt water and split or woven whole.

As well as weaving these typical Polynesian fish-traps, the Hawaiians used *'ie'ie* mesh in two unique, culturally important inventions: helmets (*mahiole*) and gourd baskets.

The ancient Hawaiian wore no hat; he was amply protected by his thick hair. When the conch shell trunpet resounded a call to battle, however, the chiefs adorned themselves with a high-crested, ornamental helmet. A practical head-piece, it resisted heavy blows on account of its tightly plaited rootlet framework. Over this was fitted a net of fine *oloná* cord, to which feathers were painstakingly attached. As befits a ruler or chief, the helmet was designed in royal colors: red and gold with sweeping lines of black or green. In form they suggested a Greek origin but were independently derived. There is nothing like them anywhere else.

Of all their skills, the Hawaiians excelled most in featherwork; this is a fact recognized worldwide. Their artistry in designing and stitching the fabulously rich and intricate cloaks and helmets were admired, and still are, not only by the general public, but by museum curators everywhere.

Basketware coverings for gourds (see drawing) were similarly uniquely Hawaiian; they must have risen out of practical necessity. As we have mentioned before, gourds and wooden bowls were the chief containers used in old Hawaii, undoubtedly because woven items such as coconut platters would not hold poi too well. Because gourds are brittle and crack easily, it is only sensible that the Hawaiians would experiment with strong, close-fitting containers in which to transport them. So they used *'ie'ie*, producing quite an array of curiously shaped gourd carriers. Some were

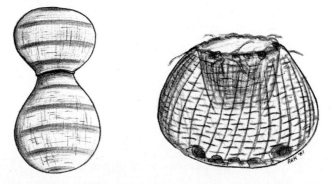

Gourd basket-carrier and fishing trap, both woven from 'ie'ie rootlets.   **61**

coarsely twined, others finely woven; they varied from round and squat to tall and dumb-bell or bottle-shaped.

Normally Hawaiians did not wear shoes either; the callouses on their soles were sufficiently leathery to substitute as shoes. However, when it was necessary to cross jagged lava, sandals woven from 'ie'ie leaves were indispensable, and were actually preferred to white man's footgear as pioneer botanist David Douglas attested. During his ascent of Mauna Loa (Big Island) in 1834, Douglas noted that even though he had supplied shoes for his native guides, "none of them could walk when so equipped, preferring a sole mat, made of tough ('ie'ie) leaves, and fastened round the heel and between the toe, which seemed indeed to answer the purpose entirely well."

Even the 'ie'ie's stems had their uses; young shoots provided tonics and older stems made cordage. And, as the leading quote suggests, leaves were occasionally used to thatch huts.

From its natural habit of twining around trees, interconnecting every stratum of the forest from the ground to the canopy, 'ie'ie represents the intertwining of many aspects of Hawaiian living. It assisted in the provision of their basic protein, fish, and carried around their staple starch, poi. It protected a chief's head during war, additionally presenting him with an air of nobility and power. Whenever a religious event was celebrated, 'ie'ie was among the decorations.

Weaving this sinuous vine and sewing over it feathers from the birds that flitted among its leaves and partook of its crimson fruits, the Hawaiians rose to their ultimate heights in craftsmanship.

Scientific Name: Freycinetia arborea
Other names: 'ie'ie and *kiekie* (both used all over Polynesia for related species)
Family: Pandanaceae or screwpine family; about 156 species; related to true palms.

Rat and O'u eating 'ie'ie fruit.

C. Kepler

Ridgetop 'ie'ie *amidst treeferns and* kanawao (Broussaisia arguta*).*

Tasty 'ie'ie *fruits are relished by rats.*

W. Mull

*Damselfly nymph (*Megalagrion *sp.) is adapted to living on* 'ie'ie's *long pleated leaves.*

63

'ILIMA

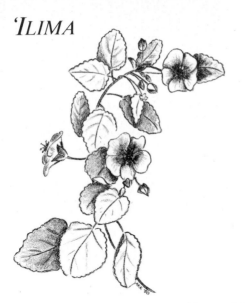

Royal 'ilima: *golden blossoms for lei-threading.*

It is summer, 1810. Residents of Lahaina, Maui, are greatly anticipating the festivities surrounding the imminent marriage of their chief's daughter to a young man of noble birth from Kauai. Families are scattering from shore to forest performing assigned tasks: catching fish, evaporating salt; preparing dogs, pigs and chickens; gathering *limu* (seaweed), *ti* leaves and *maile;* catching birds; stringing *kukui* nuts on long coconut fibres for lighting; and practicing hula. Several ladies have been instructed to gather *'ilima* flowers to string into leis for the chief's numerous relatives.

Although *'ilima* grows naturally in the surrounding scrub-forest, the ladies choose to pick higher quality flowers from a cultivated patch of plants upslope towards the deeply-carved valleys of West Maui. Gathering their baskets (lined with *ti* leaves to keep the flowers fresh) they set off into the arid countryside. Before leaving their thatched huts, they snip off many lengths of fine white *olonā* fiber with a freshly sharpened bamboo knife, in readiness for making the leis later.

One grandmother requests the ladies to pick some whole cotton flowers to mix with *'ilima* and grated coconut for her stomach trouble. Another warns them to watch out for the Goddess Laka (goddess of the hula), who sometimes manifests unexpectedly as an *'ilima* bush.

After a gentle climb, the ladies have soon plucked thousands of richly colored, golden flowers. Each blossom resembles a small hibiscus with five, slightly crinkled petals arranged around a short central tube studded with stamens. They are so abundant that their ladies' baskets are inadequate, so they hastily weave some temporary baskets by braiding together whole plants, keeping the roots uppermost for handles.

Into other bags they place flowers and buds to crush for laxatives for the village babies. Everything accomplished, they are back in Lahaina by dusk. Early next morning they busily occupy themselves stringing orange floral cylinders – truly "royal leis".

They verbally toss around a riddle: "In the evening, gathered; in the morning, pierced; in the forenoon, hung in the air." Answer: "An *'ilima lei.*" They also chat about how the royal color changed from scarlet to gold soon after the white

West Maui's foothills, for centuries a favored locality for picking 'ilima flowers.

K. Kepler

man arrived. How striking these leis will appear on the chief's family, they surmise, especially on the chief, who will be wearing his golden cape of rare *mamo* feathers!

Distributed throughout the Pacific and in China, *'ilima,* a diminutive member of the hibiscus family, once held the title of Hawaii's national flower before its larger, dark pink cousin (*kokio 'ula*) usurped it. *'Ilima* now holds a lesser distinction, the flower of Oahu.

As you drive around the leeward coasts of all Hawaii's major islands, you will undoubtedly note that *'ilima* is quite common is places, generally growing from one to three feet high. Adapted to dry areas, sometimes existing under harsh conditions of poor soil and intense heat, it varies greatly. It may flourish in *aa* lava, pure sand, or in soil among grasses. In moister valleys, the *'ilima's* heart-shaped scalloped leaves (similar in shape to the houseplant, swedish ivy), grow to two or three times their normal size. I have seen lush plants over six feet tall in Olowalu Valley, Maui, for instance, that could almost be called shrubs. Their gray-green, downy leaves in some locations are so soft they are almost velvety. Feel some! Once again we see a plant adapted to conserving water by having its leaves covered with whitish hairs.

All of the above examples of *'ilima* were termed *'ilima kula* by the Hawaiians. The most frequently encountered wild form, this type has flowers that are small, yellow and sometimes of irregular shape. Their long woody stems were occasionally used for building slats, but the flowers were rarely utilized.

Royal 'ilima (*'ilima lei*) is the cultivated variety most often used for leis. Its relatively large (about 1'' diameter) flowers are a darker orange-yellow and much more attractive than the wild type.

The third, and last, form of *'ilima* is a little creeper (*'ilima papa*) that barely exceeds two inches in height. Mat-like, it provides a charming ground cover along arid roadsides and some beaches. Previously an abundant plant, much of its habitat has now been usurped by sugar plantations and development. However, it may still be met with in many places such as Kaena Point (Oahu), Kaupo area (Maui), Moomomi Beach (Molokai), and in most botanical gardens.

'Ilima plants are easy to transplant from the wild or grow from seed. Traditionally Hawaiians embedded an *opihi* (limpet) shell under the young transplant in order that the mature plant have "the firmness of an *opihi*". Whether or not you deem this

'Ilima, *flower of Oahu, worn proudly.*

R. McDonald

necessary, you mightlike to try a plant or two in your garden. They require practically no care and will provide bright, miniature hibiscus-like flowers for you the whole year.

'Ilima has been loved for centuries. Its blossoms were so cherished for leis that it was one of the few non-food plants cultivated by ancient Hawaiians. Even up to the 20th Century (when women still had plenty time and patience), *'ilima* leis were given to departing friends, as this reputedly brought good luck. A good time to see these is May/Lei Day, especially on Oahu. Being laborious to make (each lei requires about 500 flowers), today's trend is to replace fresh flowers by circles of closely-strong crepe paper!

Songs were written about it too, such as the following "Beautiful *'Ilima*", composed by Princess Emma Alexandria De Fries around 1870:

> *"This flower is softly fragrant*
> *And quickly secured.*
> *Lovely when pelted by the dew.*
> *O Beautiful 'ilima,*
> *Choice of my heart.*
> *O sweet and charming flower*
> *Soft and lovely to behold."*

In old Hawaii, as in many other countries, yellow and gold were, and still are, special colors. Bright, intricately stitched featherwork and *'ilima* leis were fashionable golden items. Today the birds (*o'o* and *mamo*) which supplied these feathers are virtually extinct, but *'ilima,* although not exactly a "high quality plant", is still plentiful. Its pretty, sunny flowers help us appreciate the small portion of our cultural heritage associated with these esteemed colors.

Scientific Name: Sida fallax ("a deceiving nymph")
Family: Hibiscus or Malvaceae; about 1000 species; related to hibiscus, hau, milo, cotton, okra.

K. Kepler

Creeping 'ilima, a charming mat-like ground cover that favors beaches and arid, lowland soils.

66

I R O N W O O D

K. Kepler

K. Kepler

Iron-like roots: potential shark-hooks.

Drooping stem-clusters ("leaves") embellish coasts.

A bronzed Tahitian man is busily engaged in a grove of ironwood trees. After carefully examining many roots, he chooses a young, smooth, partly exposed one, free from protuberances, then slowly twists and bends it into a U-shape. He ties it to a larger root with some coconut sennit, then continues his search for other suitable lengths of root.

The first white men to observe this ancient custom were baffled. Their amazement increased when, after trading nails with natives, they discovered them bent and partly buried in the ground!

To Pacific people unfamiliar with metal, ironwood was one of the hardest substances known; it even sank in water. Its wood was of particular importance in the construction of fish-hooks, along with bone, ivory, turtle shell and mullusc shells. In the above ingenious manner, men were able to control the size and shape of their one-piece, potential fish-hooks. When the chosen root was sufficiently large, a man severed it from the parent tree, removed the soft outer bark, sanded and polished it (using coral and sharkskin), then finally oiled it with coconut oil to a high gloss. The ensuing hard shiny hooks ranged from small fine ones to formidable shark hooks measuring over one inch thick and 15 inches long. It is no wonder that the Polynesians, so dependent upon the sea, should eagerly trade pigs and vegetables for white man's strange, unbreakable substance! What better use for a nail than to plant it to grow into a sturdy fish-hook?

Ironwood, occurring naturally in Australia (hence the name "Australian pine") and South-East Asia, was carried over vast stretches of the Pacific hundreds of years ago by the earliest Polynesians. It developed a fascinating cultural lore. Tahitians believed that these trees sprang from the bodies of fallen warriors – their blood became its red sap and their hair, the stringy "leaves". To carry a piece of wood in one's canoe was a sure invitation for storms and unfavorable winds.

In addition to growing fish-hooks, ironwood was carved into high quality weapons. Ironwood became so intimately associated with war that whenever trees were felled one automatically assumed that war was imminent.

This association with war is also reflected in language; throughout Polynesia the word for ironwood, *tea,* is synonymous with that for warrior and bravery.

Associated with this was the belief that ironwood weapons possessed *mana* (supernatural powers). Spears and clubs could gain *mana* from their users, and vice versa. Fighters dipped them in the blood of slain enemies to increase their *mana* and gain more prestige for themselves. Some were handed down through generations until they became so dangerous that they had to be protected in special huts! To us today, these weapons look pretty frightening, even without their *mana.* Take, for example, the multiple-edged swords (see drawing) made from ironwoods forked branches. These were used for disembowelling enemies. You just ripped and sawed them across somebody's naked loins!

Ironwood's iron-like wood was also carved into tapa-beaters and tool-handles.

In Hawaii we find that this rich Polynesian heritage is absent. Hawaiians used ironwood for firewood but little else. The reason, I believe, is simple. Early Hawaiians did not bring this tree here, and by the time it became established (about 100 years ago) it was too late for it to be of any importance culturally. Even its Hawaiian name, *paina* ("pine") indicates its relatively recent arrival, as there were no true pines in our islands prior to the 19th Century.

Interestingly, a new and more peaceful cultural use has arisen in Hawaii. The "warrior tree", instead of symbolizing war, now denotes marital fidelity! Early Japanese immigrants, missing Japanese pines, began to use sprigs of ironwood for their New Year festival decorations. This use commemorated an ancient couple, Matsue and Teoyo, whose love under the pines increased as each year progressed.

The ironwood's resemblance to shaggy, drooping pines, however, is only superficial, despite its long "needles" and small "cones". For example, the slender green "needles" that hang and wave in the breeze are actually pendant, jointed stems. If you pick one up, note that around each joint (node) project several minute teeth, its true leaves, degenerated almost to invisibility.

Perhaps you have admired a sunset through an ironwood's drooping foliage, perhaps you have cursed its spiky fallen cones as you walked bare-footed at certain beaches.... It *is* rather drab and a bit out of place in the "lush" tropics, but it is a useful tree, especially in arresting coastal erosion. A hardy product of millions of years of evolution, it is able to survive under harsh, salty, dry and windy conditions, braving storms and burning sun with equal stalwartness.

Scientific Name: Casuarina equisetifolia
Other names: Common casuarina, false ironwood,
she-oak, Australian pine, *paina*
Family: Casuarinaceae or Casuarina family; about
25 species. Not closely related to any
other family; about five species of introduced casuarinas in Hawaii.

Shark-tooth weapon.

Ironwood leaves.

K. Kepler

*'luffy lemon powder-puffs brighten spring-
ime.*

K. Kepler

Dawn highlights a koa *gully.*

KOA

Spring is here! In Hawaii it does not exhibit its powerful glory as a three-dimensional carpet of brilliance and a symphony of sounds, transforming cold gray landscapes into a kaleidoscope of color, as in the temperate regions. It is more subtle. Nature nudges us gently, adding to the abundance of beauty already here. A *koa* tree bursts forth with masses of yellow pompoms. The *ama'uma'u* treefern unfolds new pink-bronzy fiddleheads in youthful radiance. Native *amakihi* sing bubbly songs in the uplands while at the beach golden plovers (*kolea*) change into their courtship attire, adding gold spangles to their fawn feathers and turning their breasts black before flying to Alaska to breed.

In a few weeks such changes pass. Some will have noticed them. A horseback rider in Waimea or Olinda relishes the engaging aroma of new blue eucalyptus leaves; a jogger in upcountry Maui cannot help but admire the splendid mauve jacaranda flowers, and goat-hunters in dry forests imbibe drafts of air gently scented with *koa's* blossoming sweetness.

It is not as easy to find *koa* now as formerly, even though it was the second most abundant tree in Hawaii's native forest. Unfortunately, medium-elevation lands where *koa* grow, enjoying moderate rainfall and well-drained soils, made prime ranching areas. Thus vast acreages have been chopped down or grazed over. Some of our most picturesque country is in these *mauka* pasturelands that were once dense *koa* forests.

Koa possess two types of leaves depending on their age. Seedlings grow finely divided leaves (resembling *koa haole* and wattles) that are so different from the curved mature leaves that many people do not recognize them as *koa*. The transition between leaf types is gradual, and after the tree is a few feet high you can usually find the two leaf-types on a single twig. Actually the gracefully curving adult "leaves" are not true leaves at all, but flattened, expanded leaf-stalks. This is obvious during the transition phase. Mature leaves, especially when fresh, are often covered with a fine, talcum-like powder, which undoubtedly prompted the name of a legendary Kauai girl, Kail-lau-o-ke-koa, "the beautiful one with skin as soft as a *koa* leaf".

Koa is sometimes confused with Australian eucalypts which also have curved leaves. They often occur together. (If you are in doubt, tear up a leaf; the eucalyptus will have the familiar "Vicks" smell and cup-shaped seedpods, as opposed to a "leafy" smell and long seedpods of *koa*.) Captain Cook, the first white man to see *koa,* was quick to note this superficial resemblance: "There are only two kinds of trees, which can properly be denominated timber," he writes as he walks in the grand *koa* forests above Kealekekua Bay, Big Island, "the first, in the shape of its leaves, bears a strong resemblance to the spice trees of Van Diemen's land (i.e. Australian eucalypts), and grows to a great height; of this the natives make their canoes."

Four years later (1792), botanist Menzies made the same observation. I mention this because, ironically, it was this very botanist who proudly introduced cattle to Hawaii. In his desire to provide fresh meat to travelers and help the natives, he failed to foresee how these large mammals would devastate Hawaii's native forests, including hundreds of endemic species that he was collecting so avidly. Today he would shed many apologetic tears if he could witness the present condition of *koa* forests (largely a result of cattle) or read a list of Hawaii's endangered plant species!

Koa's pollen-laden blossoms mature into brown, bean-like seedpods. No-one knows how the relatively heavy, non-bouyant ancestral seed could have made its way here from their probable homelands, Australia or Mauritius Island (near Africa), where grow today the *koa's* closest relatives.

Possibly the most ancient tree species in our island chain, *koa* is a real *kama'aina* (old-timer) of millions of years' standing. We know this because nearly 50 species of endemic insects live on *koa,* many never leaving its protective folds. This number of native insects is greater than for any other Hawaiian plant. The Polynesian introduced coconut palm, in contrast, harbors no native insects.

Bird studies also indicate that *koa* evolved early in Hawaii's geological history. Several species of Hawaiian finches are (and were) associated primarily or exclusively with *koas*. Unfortunately all are either extinct or extremely rare now. The orange Greater Koa Finch, last observed in 1896, lived on the Big Island, spending most of its time in the crowns of lofty *koa* feeding on green seedpods. Its huge bill, strong jaw muscles and tough digestive system were specially modified to cope with big hard seeds. Bird and *koa* evolved together as inseparable companions.

Such birds may be as essential to the welfare of *koa* forests as *koa* are essential to them. Just as any community is dependent on the co-operation and interaction of all its members, so is a *koa* forest dependent upon its constellation of birds, plants, spiders, insects, and fungi for survival. When such natural interactions are disturbed the forests suffer. Similarly, it is difficult to duplicate Nature's balance in a *koa* plantation – for almost 50 years foresters have borne many heartaches trying to raise *koa* on a commercial scale.

As spring arives in the *koa* forest many subtle events become apparant. Birds find certain types of large caterpillars for their chicks; a native butterfly finds nourishment in the powder-puff blossoms. A staggering number of other minute details keep the forest healthy, just as a staggering number of chemical processes maintain our own bodily health. Spring, to whatever degree we are aware of it, is out annual reminder of the complexities of life at all levels.

Youth in transition to maturity.

Fine mists swirl around the precipitous cliffs of Nuuanu Valley, Oahu, and move rapidly seaward, engulfing successive tracts of lush, pristine rain forest on their way. Kahiko, a friend, and a *kahuna* (priest) don their bulky, but effective, *ti*-leaf raincoats and continue plodding along an indistinct muddy track towards a small valley adjoining the upper reaches of the main valley. Their destination is an exceptionally fine stand of majestic *koa* trees, Hawaii's largest native tree. Ever since he was a boy, Kahiko had accompanied his father up to these tall, stately *koa*, trimming unhealthy branches and clearing away unwanted weeds and shrubs. Now it is time to select one of these "family" trees for a new fishing canoe. Although *koa* trees are abundant on Oahu, many have twisted trunks and wide-spreading branches creating picturesque shapes, aesthetically beautiful but unsuitable for canoes. As they traverse a steep mountain ridge, barefooted, the men keep a sharp lookout for an auspicious bird, the *'elepaio*, whose presence will soon become of utmost importance to their activities. A variety of scolds and whistles soon reveal the *'elepaio's* presence, and a small brown and white, speckled bird alights daintily on a nearby twig. Perkily and inquisitively, it cocks and fans its tail, flitting about in a friendly manner. A good omen, the men comment, especially as it follows them a short distance to their chosen *koa* tree.

Beneath this giant, 97′ tall and 4′ in diameter, the party deposit their meagre belongings, simple tools of stone, wood and shell; foods wrapped in *ti*-leaf bundles, sun-dried fish, tapa, and animals for sacrifice. The kahuna begins chanting to Kupulupulu, god of the *koa* forest. This god presides over men and all creatures present, either temporarily or permanently, in the koa forest. Every wanderer is in his domain; every rustle is heard and judged accordingly by his acute ears. The men respect the forest, its inhabitants, and its unseen powers. The kahuna, with his incantations and offerings, acts as a mediator between Kupulupulu and the men, lessening the latter's fears.

As the hefty men chop away at the *koa's* base with their stone adzes, they utter:

O Ku Akua (O God), Take care while the tree is falling,
Do not break our boat,
Do not let the tree smash and crack."

K. Kepler

The best ukeleles are manufactured from native koa.

Charming koa *forest, NW Kauai.*

Many hours later, the enormous trunk trembles, its sickle-shaped leaves and sturdy branches rustle and creak, and a taboo of silence falls on the party as they scoot away. With a sharp crackle of breaking wood followed by a resounding crash, the *koa* tumbles to the ground, its fall eased as it smashes through the shrubs. The formerly peaceful atmosphere is disturbed, and birds scatter. The men wait for the *'elepaio* to check out the quality of this veteran *koa* log. The *'elepaio* is actually Goddess Lea, wife of the chief god of canoe-makers, in disguise. Swiftly the little bird springs onto the fallen log as the men stand by with bated breaths. Hopping around, poking here and there, it spends much time grabbing at spiders, beetles and caterpillars gleaned from cracks in the bark.

Sorrowfully, the kahuna announces that the *'elepaio* has made its decision. *Auwe!* (Too bad!) The men understand. This magnificent *koa* is useless; it harbors defects; their canoe cannot be constructed from it despite the fact that Kahiko has tended it for 32 years. They must choose another.

Leaving it to rot, they muster renewed strength to check out another favored tree and then return home to their village near our present Honolulu. Three days later, with a fresh black pig and other offerings, they carefully repeat all the proscribed procedures; this time the gods smile somewhat more favorably. The Goddess Lea, disguised as another *'elepaio,* flies to the fallen log, inspects it briefly by tapping the wood and, finding no food, runs directly from one end to the other, whistling. Good... the ultimate sign has now been given. After more offerings, chants and omens, the men continue the numerous operations necessary to eventually finish the months-long project. As the work continues over the next weeks, chopping off the crown and lateral branches, shaping with fire and adzes, and hauling out of the forest with thick ropes, several *'elepaio* stay closeby, constantly gleaning from adjacent vegetation, guarding the laborers, and blessing the canoe during each phase of its construction. Once down in the village, there is finer carving to do, sandpapering with coral and sharkskin, dyeing, caulking, varnishing, and naturally, more rituals. Eventually the basic *koa* hull receives its outrigger and other attachments and is ready for many years of fishing service to the owners.

The paramount importance of *'elepaio* in the making of *koa* canoes is a very interesting cultural point from an ornithologist's perspective. *'Elepaio* eat insects, and if they find many, it may mean that the trunk has cracks and defects, not the best for a sound canoe. Hence the omen is that of a "bad" tree. If the bird merely hops around and finds no insects, then the tree is more likely to be "good".

Also, *'elepaio* have never been seen or heard on Maui, yet the largest double canoes ever reported originated in Maui's Kipahulu Valley. Each hull measured 120' long and 9' deep! Could such canoes have been constructed without propitiations to,

72

Hand-carved outrigger canoe, a reminder of past and present seafarers. City of Refuge, Is. of Hawaii.

World's largest koa, Keahou ranch, Is. of Hawaii.

and omens from, Goddess Lea, the *'elepaio?*

The ancient Hawaiians recognized *koa* as a high quality wood. Its straight bole and close grain which did not warp, even after years in sea-water, was invaluable. Fishing was important to them, as fish formed the greater part of their protein intake. As Hawaii has few protective reefs, such as are found in many more southern islands, the Hawaiians needed large, sturdy canoes that could withstand the rigors of our windy, choppy channels and surrounding ocean. Thus, even though twelve other trees were used for canoes, *koa* was preferred above all.

Koa wood also made the long heavy surfboards used by royalty. It did not make good calabashes though, as the wood imparted a strange taste to *poi.* Other uses included canoe paddles, dyes from the bark, and medicines from the leaves. The early Portuguese made the first ukeleles out of *koa* too.

Certain types of dreams prophesied past and future events in the ancient culture. To have a *koa* dream was considered beneficial. The best dream was to see *koa* growing taller than all other types of trees around, and to see one great koa extending high above all. The fine growth of *koa* represented wealth; other trees signified friends that gathered around a person when he was wealthy.

For the old Hawaiians, *koa* were long-lived monarchs of the forest, protected by one of their lesser, but nonetheless powerful, gods. Even the native name, meaning "bold, brave, fearless, and warrior" reflects this respect.

E ole koa: ..... let him live, with the health, wealth and well-being of a *koa* tree!

Scientific Name: Acacia koa
Family: Leguminosae or legume family, about 12,000 species; related to beans, kiawe.

Double-hulled koa canoe.

Kukui *blossoms: ingredient of old herbal remedies.*

K. Kepler

Pale foliage of kukui highlights lowland vegetation.

KUKUI

Two Hawaiian fishermen paddle slowly towards the open waters beyond Kaneohe Bay, Oahu, Fairly strong winds are blowing across a mild swell, producing a choppy sea. Visibility if poor, so one man pulls some partly-roasted *kukui* nuts from a covered gourd, chews on them one at a time and spits the mixture onto the water surface. The surrounding portion of ocean becomes smooth almost instantly, providing a clearer window through which to see fish, especially the gaudy blue and green parrotfish (*uhu*), their anticipated prey.

Their nets, carefully folded in the bottom of the canoe, have just been tanned with a fresh reddish-brown stain made from *kukui* bark. They check these nets and their *kukui* fishing torch for the final time, then reach for some snacks as they slowly head further away from shore.

Paddling takes energy, and a little later we find them munching on shreds of pork, *poi,* and *inamona.* The latter is a spicy relish concocted from pounded, roasted *kukui* nuts, sea-salt and dried squid ink-bags. Although it doesn't sound too appetizing, *inamona* was popular in olden days, and is still available from stores today, although it is expensive. Nowadays the *kukui* nuts are usually mixed with red hot peppers instead of squid ink-bags.

The above story merely scratches the surface of the innumerable uses of Hawaii's official State tree, the *kukui.* From leaves, trunk, bark, nuts, sap and flowers, our ancestors (or adopted ancestors, whichever the case may be) gathered materials for fishing, housing, tattooing, ornamentation and rituals.

Tall or short, often branching grotesquely like an old oak, *kukui* may attain

100' in stature. Their characteristic pale green, maple-like leaves (having three to seven points) contrast greatly with the darker foliage of other forest trees. The *kukui's* young foliage is especially bright and silvery due to a hairy, almost powdery covering.

Isabella Bird, a courageous, enthusiastic traveler around and within our islands in the 19th Century, describes this picturesque leafage in the following manner: "It presents a mass of foliage quite unique, giving the gulch the appearance as if billows of green had rolled in and solidified there."

How poetic! Yet how aptly is describes those pale green mounds nestling in and around the bottoms of our lush lowland valleys.

Although generally considered native to Hawaii, the *kukui* is another of our "characteristic forest trees" that did not reach here of its own accord. Despite the fact that it fits in so well with the native vegetation and appears as though it has been here for millions of years, the *kukui* was brought here only about 1500 years ago by the early Hawaiians.

Polynesians, bound for Hawaii, had used and cherished this useful tree in the Marquesas and Society Islands and, before sailing to far-off islands, added its seeds to their collection of coconuts, taro rhizomes, miscellaneous plant cuttings, pigs and chickens. In addition to its potential value in their new homeland, *kukui* nuts served as hog food on these long ocean voyages.

Farther back in history, the *kukui* originated in Asia, becoming distributed throughout the pacific by even earlier Polynesian seafarers, ancestors of both French Polynesians and Hawaiians. If you pick up a *kukui* nut it is easy to understand why such a heavy fruit needed to be transported by man. Drop one in seawater and it will sink in a few days. As the nuts decay they become more bouyant, but a rotten seed is of little value in colonizing a distant island!

One of the ways in which biologists can tell if a tree is native or not is to examine the number of native insects associated with it. Longtime Hawaiian residents such as *koa* and *'ohi'a* harbor close to 50 species of native insects each. A more "recent *kama'aina*" (old-timer) such as *kukui,* which has only lived here about 1500 years, has not had enough time to develop a specific native insect population. How many do we find? Only *one*! That's just a little less than the number on the banana plant, and a little more than the number on coconut, other relative newcomers to Hawaii.

The *kukui's* major use in early Hawaiian domestic life was in lighting. Using traditional methods, these dark-skinned Pacific people knew how to fashion three types of lights from *kukui* nuts. (Actually the Hawaiian word *kukui* means "lamp" or "light", and the English name, "candlenut" also alludes to this use.)

These ingenious lighting devices fascinated early explorers and travelers. They never failed to inspire written comments in diaries and ship's logs. As an example, David Samwell, surgeon's mate aboard Captain Cook's vessels, recorded the following in 1779, while visiting the Hawaiian Islands: "For lights in their homes they burn the same oily nuts placed in a row upon sticks that they do at Otaheite (Tahiti) and the friendly isles (Tonga)."

These "candles"? "Shish kebabs" of roasted kukui nuts! Each one consisted of 10-12 roasted, shelled *kukui* nuts threaded on a central core (see drawing). Either the stiff, flexible midribs of coconut leaflets or slivers of bamboo were used for this thin column. After the nut was lighted it burned for two or three minutes with a yellow flame and slightly fragrant smoke.

Candle.

C. Kepler

Twisted kukui *trunks characterize many lush valleys.*   *Oil-lamp and fishing torch.*

During the evenings, as adults sat inside their grass huts "talking story", children tended the lights. While the top nut burnt, a child inverted the "candle" to light the next nut, and so on down the line. After each inversion the "candle" was replaced in its stone receptacle to keep it upright. Children must have been constantly hopping up and down attending to this time-consuming duty!

At larger social gatherings such as outdoor dancing or night fishing, this general idea was expanded into an *aulama* or torch. Here several "candles" were bound together and enclosed in a sheaf of *ti* leaves. The whole thing was then secured to a bamboo handle (see diagram above). This fiery cylinder, measuring three to six inches in diameter and up to four feet in length, emitted abundant acrid smoke, which, in addition to the obvious safety factor, rendered it unsuitable for burning inside grass-thatched huts.

Royalty utilized the next state in the evolution and refinement of lights. All the work was left, as usual, to village commoners, who crushed large quantities of roasted *kukui* nuts in stone mortars. They then gave the expressed oil to the chiefs. A small portion of this oil was poured into a small stone with a hollowed-out depression on its upper surface. After adding the final touch, a strip of twisted tapa (bark-cloth), the lamp was ignited. It burnt unattended for hours. (These stone lamps resembled the first European ones, which utilized olive oil or beef tallow, independent inventions from totally different cultures.) They work too; we have friends on Oahu who use them for a special Hawaiian touch at dinner parties.

Kukui oil is not a low-grade, "primitive" oil. Akin to linseed oil, it penetrates deeply, dries quickly, and is particularly effective on wood. Some early foreigners on Oahu established small businesses by extracting *kukui* oil. All the nuts were hand-gathered, and despite crude manufacturing methods, annual exports reached 10,000 gallons between 1840 and 1850.

Prolific nut-producers, a *single acre* of *kukui* trees yielded an estimated five tons of nuts and 237 gallons of oil! However, as labor costs rose steadily gathering nuts became unprofitable. It is interesting to note that all this oil was sold to Russian traders for use in their settlements on the north-west coast of America.

The *kukui's* bark is also very useful, being rich in tannins. Infusions from this bark were utilized greatly in the 19th Century for tanning hides. The red-brown stain produced a high-grade, durable leather. The early Hawaiians were undoubtedly aware of these tanning properties as they used *kukui* bark infusions to preserve their fish-nets. These tannins must also have produced a "high', as one of Hawaii's early missionaries, Lorenzo Lyons, (mid-19th Century), noted (with great disdain) that "bits of *kukui* bark were a popular adjunct to one's liquor."

On account of its multiplicity of uses and "distinctive beauty of its light green foliage which embellishes many of the slopes of our beloved mountains", the *kukui* was designated on May 1, 1959, as the official symbol of *Hawaii nei.*

Tears welled up in the eyes of the strong Hawaiian prince, but he dared not cry. The pain was excruciating and he felt increasingly weak as more and more blood streamed from his back. His father once again dipped the sharply-pointed bird bones into the burnt *kukui* nut mixture. Then the boy experienced even more pain as the neddle-sharp bones pierced his strong skin in several more places. That was enough... he felt faint now. He would have to wait until tomorrow.

Historically one of man's most agonizing, self-inflicted tortures, tattooing was once widespread in Polynesia. The ancient Hawaiians used two mixtures to produce permanent skin marks; the most commonly used one utilized *kukui* nuts. Fine soot, scraped from smooth beach stones beneath a fire of *kukui* nuts, was mixed with oil or coconut water. The instrument dipped in this dye was fashioned from fish or albatross bones mounted on a wooden handle. It was positioned on the skin, then struck sharply with a mallet. The spiked points pricked and penetrated the skin, producing a series of blue-black dots which eventually formed the desired pattern.

A few years ago my husband and I talked to several youths in Western Samoa, where tattooing, using ancient methods and kukui nut dyes, is still practiced. Generally metal tools are used now, but in some outlying areas mounted fish-bones are still employed. It is like reliving pages of history to hear first-hand accounts of their tattooing ordeals. After two to seven weeks of daily pricking with these sharp instruments, the youths need to convalesce for at least four months. During this period their skin rises up to form huge, ugly welts. They feel very weak through loss of large amounts of blood and are incapable of even simple physical work. One boy related the story of a friend who died while undergoing tattooing; his body could not fight off the massive infection that resulted.

Yet to stop half-way through the process brings lifelong disgrace, not only to the youth involved, but to his extended family too. Shame is very difficult to endure in Samoa today, and undoubtedly this was true also in old Hawaii.

(It may be of interest to note here that our modern word "tattoo" is derived from the Tahitian *tatu.* Early Western sailors admired this form of Polynesian art so greatly that they carried the idea back to Europe with them, anglicizing the local term en route.)

Another rather bizarre use of *kukui* in former Hawaiian eras was in the detection of criminals! This also relates to the concept of shame, and illustrates the tremendous influence of the *kahuna* (priests) on all classes of people. Say a valuable article had been stolen. A *kahuna* would be requested to assist in unearthing the offender. He broke a *kukui* nut, threw it into a small fire and uttered an incantation, declaring that the thief should be killed. If the offender appeared and made restitution, he was severely punished and set free. If not, the *kahuna* repeated this ceremony twice more. During the third round, the high chief would proclaim across the island that the guilty one had been prayed to death. So bound by fear and belief in the super-

C. Kepler

K. Kepler

Billows of pale green nestle in gulches.

Samoan youth tattooed with kukui *stain.*

natural were the old Hawaiians, that often the thief actually withered away and died as a consequence of these rituals.

Products of the *kukui* tree were also used medicinally, usually by another type of *kahuna,* the "medicine man" (*kahuna lapa'au*). Sap from young twigs treated a variety of sores, rashes, blisters and chapped lips, especially in young children. Some kama'ainas alive today have told me that they used such medicines on their children many years ago. One old prescription for a mouthgargle instrusts one to grind *kukui* blossoms with the bark from *kukui* and *'ohi'a* trees. You strain this, add salt and coconut water and use when necessary. I haven't tried it, but it doesn't sound too unpleasant!

Of interest to surf-enthusiasts is the manner in which *kukui* helped to preserve surfboards, which, as we all know, were invented by Hawaiians. Teenagers, who had to lug around those old-fashioned, heavy, long boards, used to rub the same mixture that was used for tattooing, into the wood. After thorough staining and drying, they applied several coats of pure *kukui* oil, which penetrated deeply, preventing premature rot. There was no fiberglass or surfboard wax in those days!

Kukui trees had so many uses it is impossible to enumerate them. Hawaiians loved to scatter them throughout their villages, not only for their usefulness, but also for shade, beauty, and perhaps because they attracted birds. People chanted about *kukui,* clinging to memories of particular places or loved ones. One forgotten lady, lamenting for her lost husband, found solace in the following verses:

> *"My companion of the rain, of the returning water....*
> *My companion of night and day....*
> *My companion in the* kukui *grove of Ko'olau...."*

Some groves were famous for their "fragrant sweet nuts" which supplied royalty. Others provided shade and mulch for taro.

Originally introduced by the early Hawaiians, the *kukui* became more and more common in our forests as the years slipped by. Pigs relished the raw nuts and disseminated their seeds far beyond village boundaries. Now a conspicuous tree in all of Hawaii's mountains, in dry gorges as well as in areas of abundant rainfall, *kukui* is easy for the novice to identify even from a distance. Watch for patches of silvery-green leaves, clusters of small whitish flowers and bunches of large, round, green, smooth-skinned nuts. Maybe your children might enjoy making leis from its leaves and flowers as children have done for centuries. The lei of Molokai is the *kukui* lei.

If you notice *kukui* blossoms floating down a mountain stream, turn your eyes towards the mountains, listen for the wind, and put back your picnic paraphernalia. Remember the old Hawaiian chant:

> *"The* kukui *blossoms foretelleth the wind;*
> *See by the people, they call for help from the wind,*
> *And warn the canoes to flee for safety."*

Patches of silvery green leaves shimmering in a windy gully beside a thundering waterfall... surfers sliding down glassy waves ... a shiny black *kukui* nut lei... spicy *inamona*... tattooing patterns... ancient stone lamps... voyaging canoes carrying snorting pigs... a "maple-leaved" house plant in your living room... the *kukui* today offers us a wealth of aesthetic beauty and past culture. No wonder it was designated our State tree!

Scientific Name: Aleurites moluccana
Other names: candlenut, *kukui*
Family: Euphorbiaceae or poinsettia family; 7,300 species; related to crotons, castor beans.

Tattooing instrument and mallet.   *Ancient Hawaiian tattoo patterns.*

K. Kepler

*Prickly-flowered cyanea (*Cyanea aculeatiflora)*, confined to a small area of East Maui.*

*Curved lobelia flowers are very evident on this bog-dweller (*Lobelia Gaudichaudii).

LOBELIAS

Dr. Perkins' heart was thumping with excitement as he crouched beneath a lacy treefern, 5,000' up in the dense rain forest of eastern Molokai. He waited a few more minutes... yes, there it was again, inserting its long curved beak into a tubular lobelia blossom dangling beneath a rosette of leaves. The shape of its bill fitted the curvature of the flower perfectly. The black bird remained a few seconds, rapidly sucking honey with its straw-like tongue. Flitting from shrub to shrub, it stayed in Dr. Perkins' general area for a short time, sipped a few droplets of water from a nearby dripping bank of moss, then disappeared.

The date was June 18, 1892. This notable naturalist was thrilled to have just discovered this new species of Hawaiian finch (formerly honeycreeper), the Black Mamo. Jet black with orange flank feathers, *mamo* were famous birds throughout the islands. Together with *o'o* they furnished millions of orange and yellow feathers so greatly valued for the stately capes worn by chiefs on ceremonial occasions.

The story of how Hawaiian finches and lobelias became so intimately associated is fascinating. Very early in Hawaii's geological history, tiny lobelia seeds arrived in our forests, probably from South America. Developing into low plants bearing smallish, tube-shaped flowers, they were pretty but not especially striking. Today's lobelias outside of Hawaii are similar to our early forms.

Some time later, small Asian finches, destined to give rise to a remarkable variety of native Hawaiian birds, also arrived in our forests. They were similarly quite ordinary (somewhat like a Cardinal) with bills that were neither large nor small, fat nor thin, long nor short, straight nor curved.

After "transplanting", conditions for both lobelias and birds were totally different from those in their respective homelands. Soils were alien, rainfall patterns varied greatly over short distances, air temperatures were warmer, humidity was greater, and even neighboring plants, birds and insects were novel. Despite this, some survived and adapted so well that their lives took a drastic turn. Both lobelias and birds proliferated and expanded, trying out different shapes according to the varied locations in which their seeds happened to germinate. Drylands, wetlands, gullies, ridges, bogs and deep forests all provided outdoor experimental laboratories for them.

Thus from lowly herbs with little blue flowers, the lobelias evolved riotously. It was as though the sky was the limit! They grew and grew.... some up to 40' high, looking like tropical palms; others branched, resembling woody candelabras and plumeria trees; others stayed small, clinging tenaciously to steep dry ridges and eventually turning into cactus-like "cabbages" with long primrose flowers. As from an artist's palette, lobelia blossoms became painted and tinted with pinks, white, reds, greens and yellows (see also front cover). Gaudy and bright or delicately tinged and striped... dozens of combinations brightened Hawaii's pristine greenery.

A number of species, not content with colorful adornment alone, added unusual textures to their flowers, leaves and stems. Knobbly protuberances, barbs, warts, fleshy spines and furrowed ridges emerged as embellishments, enhancing their eccentricity, and inspiring names such as prickly-leaved cyanea, warty clermontia, and *Cyanea horrida*. Different shaped leaves appeared, ranging from small narrow ellipses to huge, ungainly, fleshy oblongs exceeding two feet in length. Leaf margins became scalloped, pointed, fern-like or undulating.

What variety! From an estimated three original seed-types, today we know of

An extremely rare 'oha-wai (Clermontia hirsutinervis).

A rocky gulch lover with silvery bunched leaves (Lobelia grayana).

K. Kepler

A natural hybrid lobelia (Clermontia montis-loa X parviflora).

A new species of Clermontia from Molokai's elfin forests.

about 200 species. Some have only been seen once, described from a single plant tucked away somewhere in a remote valley. Were they ever common? We don't know. Some are. Occasionally these days an adventuring, sharp-eyed botanist spies a new species in an hitherto unchecked area; usually it is named after him.

Identified by their curved, tube-like flowers (up to six inches long) they are without question Hawaii's botanical treasures. (Of biogeographical interest is the fact that although Hawaii has this remarkable proliferation of lobelias, only two other species occur in the Pacific; both are in French Polynesia.)

Over time, as the lobelias changed, the birds changed too. Co-evolution: birds and flowers evolving together for mutual benefit. For example, one type of lobelia would appear in the forest, whose shape exactly fitted the bill of one type of bird. Thus the bird was assured of a food-source (nectar) and the lobelia was assured of a pollinator as the bird thrust its bill deep into its flower tube.

In the "old days", such avian behavior enabled little Hawaiian boys to catch *mamo* and other birds; they simply picked a large lobelia flower and hid in the bushes with the flower held in their fingers. When a native finch probed its long bill into the boy's flower, it would undoubtedly be quite surprised to be captured by two strong fingers grabbing the end of its bill!

Hawaiians also used the white, gluey sap from lobelia stems to brush on branches and ensnare small forest birds.

During the course of a few million years the Hawaiian finches, originating from just one ancestor, evolved into an equally spectacular array of birds of numerous shapes, sizes, colors, bill-types and feeding habits. No bird family anywhere in the world can compare with their uniqueness; they are a standard example of evolution in biology textbooks.

Many of the original Hawaiian finches, along with many lobelias, are not around today to tell their stories. With rapidly changing conditions in our forest, especially during the past 200 years, many forms of life were not able to survive the drastic changes that encroached upon their serene existences. Lobelias, with their succulent stems and fleshy leaves, were favorites of introduced wild pigs. As certain species diminished in numbers, it meant that the birds' sources of food started to disappear too, and some birds were so specialized they couldn't adapt to other foods quickly enough. The more specialized a plant or bird, the quicker it succumbed. Other factors, such as alien diseases and feather-collecting also contributed to the birds' demise.

Today about 135 of the original 200-odd lobelias, and 40 of the original 47-odd native finches (including recent subfossil finds) are either extinct, rare or endangered.

Nevertheless, those lobelias that are left are gorgeous! Strange yet unique, they are my favorite plants; it is always a delight to encounter fresh or familiar lobelioid faces in the forest. Organizations such as The Nature Conservancy and U.S. National Park Service renew our hopes for the future, as they continue with forest preservation projects which are assisting both lobelias and native birds to continue their existence for a little while longer.

Scientific Names: Cyanea, Clermontia, Rollandia, Brighamia, Delissea, Lobelia, Trematolobelia species
Other names: haha ("food of the birds"), *'oha, 'oha-wai*
Family: Lobeliaceae or lobelia family; about 700 species.

K. Kepler

Ohawai *or three clermontia, a gorgeous 2 – 3 inch, sturdy blossom (*Clermontia arborescens*).*

*Five-inch long flowers poke out from the rare "cabbage-on-a-long-stem" lobelia (*Brighamia citrina*).*

K. Kepler

Representatives of the Hawaiian finch family.

83

MAILE

Maile: *Hawaii's famous aromatic forest vine.*

"Gently floating is the fragrance (of maile),
The beauty of yon mountain."

from an old Hawaiian chant

A wedding, a luau, a visit by a dignitary. . . . let's get a *maile* lei!

Prized by the ancient Hawaiians as the noblest of all lei materials, *maile* has been respected and loved for many generations, and continues to be loved today. It was often referred to in songs, hulas, chants and dirges.

Although now associated with special occasions, *maile* leis were formerly coveted and used by all classes of people from the high chiefs down to the lowliest slaves.

One of the "sweet, odorous greens", it was used (along with ferns and wild ginger) for various ceremonies. These included bringing back spirits from the dead, house-warming parties, feasts, religious rituals and hula dancing. By far the most important of these uses was its association with hula. *Maile* was dedicated to the Goddess of the hula, Laka, and was always present on her altars. Some say it was one of the forms that she could assume at will; others that *maile* was Laka's emblem. In either event, supplications were made to this goddess, as the people of old believed that the *maile's* fragrance possessed supernatural powers. *Maile* is thus one of our heritage plants that was directly associated with gods and goddesses (other examples are *hau, hala* and *'ohi'a lehua*).

When hula dancers, adorned with *maile* anklets, wished to lift a taboo, they chanted:

C. Kepler

A wedding ceremony includes fresh maile *fashioned into traditional open-ended leis.*

"*O wildwood bouquet, O Laka!*
Hers are the growths that stand here. . .
The prayer to Laka has power;
The maile *of Laka stands to the fore.*
The maile *vine now casts its seeds.*"

In the old days you could not run or drive to a nearby florist and order a *maile* lei! Vast amounts of effort were involved in hiking up into the rugged mountains, locating patches of *maile*, hiking out again, stripping the sturdy stems with one's teeth, twisting them into a lei and finally presenting it to a loved one. No wonder such leis were cherished!

Traditionally the lei is open-ended, and because the leaves and stems are leathery and woody, it lasts several days before wilting. Most of us who have the opportunity to enjoy *maile* hang it up in the bedroom where we can smell it for weeks. The enchanting fragrance, not noticeable until the *maile's* bark is bruised, increases with age and desiccation.

The old Hawaiians took advantage of this lovely smell too. They laid *maile* (and other fragrant plants such as sandalwood) in large calabashes containing *tapa* (bark cloth). Apparently new tapa has a strange smell, so *maile* made the clothes a little more pleasant to wear.

A vine or straggling, spreading shrub, *maile* is found in native forests of our mid- to upper-elevation mountains (2000-6000′); in some places it is quite plentiful. Its long, stiff (but flexible) stems twine around each other and adjacent vegetation.

Extremely tiny flowers, born in the leaf-axils, give rise to olive-like fruits. These dark "beads" are easily spotted and avidly consumed by native birds such as thrushes (*omao*). Originally from South-east Asia, *maile* was undoubtedly spread across the vastness of the Pacific by fruit-eating birds.

Related to several of our common introduced garden ornamentals such as plumeria, oleander and allamanda, our native *maile* is also found in Samoa. The rest of the Pacific has another species. All these *maile* look very similar and, as with many Pacific plants, share similar native names and uses. For example, "*maile*" in Hawaii and Samoa translates to "*maire*" in Tahiti and the Cook Islands.

Loved for centuries, *maile* today is still regarded by everyone as a "quality native plant". Next time you hike in the mountains or visit a Botanical Garden, be sure to look them up. . . notice especially their viney growth and shiny, "mouth-shaped" paired leaves.

Remember that its lovely odor is only evident after the bark is stripped, so don't be disappointed if it does not smell as sweet as the last *maile* lei you were given!

Scientific Name: Alyxia olivaeformis
Family: Apocynaceae or periwinkle family; about 1500 species; related to plumeria, be-still tree, allamanda, oleander.

M
A
M
A
N
E

C. Kepler

Mamane *highlighted by early morning sunlight, 6,900'.*

The rain has temporarily ceased. Shafts of sunlight stream through windows of crystal-clear blue sky high up on Mauna Kea's slopes. Flitting amongst the alpine vegetation are *'amakihi* and *akiapola'au,* native Hawaiian finches. As an *'amakihi* darts between the clumped fern-like leaves of the *mamane* shrubs, his green upper parts and yellow underparts glisten like the surrounding plants. Every few seconds this little bird probes into one of the *mamane's* golden, sweet pea-like flowers to suck a tiny droplet of energy-packed nectar or grab an insect.

I watch this sun-spangled scene from a few feet away and marvel at the miracle of spring. New life-giving energy has stimulated masses of fresh, apple-green, lacy foliage on sturdy *mamane* that have withstood many past storms with remarkable stalwartness.

This is no surprise. Hard and heavy, *mamane's* yellow wood has long been prized for its straight grain and durable qualities. Formerly, Hawaiians used *mamane* posts for their best houses and also for their *o'o* (digging sticks). As metal was unknown to Polynesians before the arrival of European man, their important, and only, garden tool needed to be constructed from the hardest woods available.

In addition, when the people of old made a narrow *holua* sled for sliding down embankments, they chose the tough *mamane* wood for its runners. Even if the sled bumped into hidden rocks or other obstacles it would resist breaking, at least for a time. Incidentally, *holua* sledding was a favorite royal sport. Considering the tremendous size and weight of some of the chiefs, plus the narrowness of the sleds, it is little wonder that carpenters selected the choicest, strongest wood possible! More recently, *mamane* wood was a popular fencing material on ranches.

Mamane's presence in Hawaii, where it is found on all islands, is rather an enigma. Botanists are undecided as to how its ancestors arrived here. Its closest relative is the gorgeous *kowhai* of New Zealand, a tall striking tree which in spring is literally blanketed with golden, *mamane*-like blossoms. These give rise to long knobbly seedpods practically identical to *mamane's*. Perhaps it is too difficult to conceive of a fruit-eating bird swallowing some of these *kowhai* seeds and then getting blown out to sea and traveling 4000 miles north-eastward to Hawaii! That's awfully chancy. You might prefer the alternate theory. There is a *mamane*-like, seashore plant widespread in the Pacific called the "silver bush". Unknown from Hawaii today, it is very possible that it was the progenitor of *mamane;* thus a high

Palila *and* mamane *seedpods.*

Golden flowers and knobby seedpods: food for native birds.

mountain shrub developed from a shoreline plant no longer in existence.

Whichever speculation is correct, the seed-ancestor of our present *mamane* endured many hardships during its long passage to our isolated archipelago. It has also endured hardships since arrival and establishment here. Formerly abundant, especially on drier hill slopes, *mamane* has had to contend with many generations of browsing herbivores such as cattle, sheep and goats, who munched eagerly on its tender leaves, especially spring growth. In addition, introduced pasture grasses strangled out their seedlings.

On the Big Island, feral sheep (and formerly cattle) have ravaged many square miles of *mamane* forest on Mauna Kea, to the extent of endangering a once wide-spread, six-inch "parrot-billed" Hawaiian finch, the *palila*. Forest degradation became so serious that recently the *palila* and *mamane* became "plaintiffs" in a heated court case which dealt with the continuing existence of both parties on the vast slopes of Mauna Kea. It is encouraging to report that less than a year after the *palila* and *mamane* won their case, and a concerted effort was begun to eliminate feral sheep, the upper elevation forests began to return to their former beauty. Keikis sprouted everywhere, and old scraggly trees burst forth with renewed vigor.

On other islands, such as Molokai and Maui, numerous goat-herds (outside protected areas) continue to sap *mamane* of their life energy, and one by one, plants become brittle, topple over and die. Sometimes plants are like people, though: strong willed. *Mamane* is definitely one of these. As long as bushes can keep living and put out a few leaves, they will concentrate their energy each spring into repro-ducing seeds in a valiant effort to perpetuate themselves.

High upon the mountain, the graceful *mamane* bloom in spring (see back cover). Clothed with golden pea-like blossoms; fresh green, ferny foliage; and long knobbly seedpods dripping from their branches, they provide nectar and starch for Hawaii's unique native birds whom nature has chosen to live in their cold mountain haunts. While you are up with them, inhale some pure, cool mountain air and feel your soul become renewed with the life-giving element that spring imparts to every living thing.

Scientific Name: Sophora chrysophylla
Other names: mamane, mamani
Family: Pea or legume family, Leguminosae; about 12,000 species; related to peas, beans, *wiliwili*, kiawe, lentils, clover, monkeypod and shower trees.

Remnant mamane *forest flanks puus on Mauna K ea's volcanic slopes. Is. of Hawaii.*

Mamane *leaves and flowers.*

Goat-munched mamane *attempts to remain alive.*

Holua *sled.*

MANGO

Haden mangoes: everybody's favorite.

K. Kepler

There once was a Buddhist monk who walked into a butchershop and asked for "the very best cut of meat." The butcher replied, "Why, they're all the best!"

I like that philosophy. It teaches me to appreciate everything for its own intrinsic worth. A leg of lamb is not a pound of hamburger and shouldn't really be compared. Similarly a pineapple is not a guava is not a mango. Each is delicious and unique when freshly ripe.

I love to eat fruits daily – many kinds – but must admit that mangoes are my favorites. The texture and taste of a "Haden" mango's creamy, dazzling orange pulp is so delectably scrumptious you want to savor every bite. They are healthy for us too, packed with vitamins A and C dissolved in natural sugars. You can feel your body becoming instantly energized with their goodness.

Mango trees have long been appreciated as bearers of luscious fruits as well as providers of year-round shade. Native to India, Burma and Malaya, mangoes were some of the first fruits cultivated, supposedly as long ago as 4000 years! Long before the western world had thought of orchards and agribusiness, an Indian emperor owned and managed an enormous plantation of 100,000 mango trees. Also, around 600 B.C. an entire mango grove was presented to Buddha to cool and protect him while he meditated and taught his followers. Hindus still regard mango leaves as symbols of happiness and prosperity, using them on festive and religious occasions.

When Spanish and Portuguese traders first visited India, they too were charmed by the mango's irresistible flavor (which, incidentally, wasn't anywhere near as tasty as our improved varieties today). They spread seeds far and wide in tropical and subtropical countries. Today mangoes are grown and enjoyed wherever the climate is suitable.

The first mango seeds (of several varieties), brought to Hawaii between 1800 and 1820, did not come directly from India but from Mexico, where they had been taken

A box of luscious gold.

K. Kepler

previously by explorers. The "Hawaiian" or "common" mango is a descendent of one of these early types. This is the mango that produces the earliest fruit each year (April or May). It is best picked green and converted into chutney, as the fruit is fairly small and becomes fibrous when ripe. Wild "Hawaiian" mangoes are common in pastures, around large estates and along lowland roads.

Another old variety is the "Chinese" mango, which came here in 1885, not from China but from Jamaica! Perhaps the *pakes* preferred them to "Hawaiian" mangoes.

Many other varieties were brought to Hawaii around 1900 from Asia and the West Indies. Everybody's favorite, the "Haden", although one of the last to arrive (1930), proved to be outstandingly popular and is now found in backyard gardens more than any other variety.

Mangoes love warmth, abundant sunshine and not too much rain. It is too cold, unfortunately, for mangoes to grow above about 2,800'.

Their season lasts from May to October, depending on locality. The trees are remarkably productive. When only four years old a young tree will put out its first fruits. However, it is best to pick these off so that your tree can grow more vigorously. This may be hard, especially if you have waited anxiously for them. From the fifth to seventh year you can expect 25 to 400 lbs of fruit per tree. From then on you will have so many mangoes you won't know what to do with them all! A healthy, mature tree will grow 40 to 50 feet tall and yield an astonishing 1000 lbs of mangoes per season. (By the way, trees begun from seed and never grafted are less productive and often do not produce a true replica of the parent type.)

Some mango years are "good", others "bad". The reasons for this are twofold. It takes large amounts of energy to produce hundreds of fruit within a few months, so naturally the tree needs a bit of a break. The "Haden" tends to bear well every *two* years instead of annually. Fruit setting is also affected by climate. Excessive winter wind and rain are particularly injurious. Even though a single flower cluster may bear up to 3,000 small reddish flowers, and each tree bears hundreds of flower clusters, strong storms may ruin nearly all of them, resulting in a miserable crop of fruit.

Some people develop skin rashes from ingesting or touching parts of the mango tree. This is because mangoes are in the same family as poison ivy and poison sumac. Mango is only slightly toxic, so most people are not bothered if they avoid the sap in a mango's skin. It is best to peel the fruit, not bite directly into it as you would an apple. According to doctors, the best cure for mango rash is to apply a cortisone cream – the rash will disappear in a couple of days.

In our islands, as well as in its homeland, this delectable fruit signifies Nature's abundance, simultaneously creating happy spirits among us. During mango season nobody cares if its sticky juice exudes from our mouths and drips all over our hands and clothes! Although not a native Hawaiian plant, mangoes are a definite part of our recent heritage.

Do not all of us feel, when we see a huge spreading mango tree beside a little wooden house, especially in a rural

Shelter and fruit for isolated hunters.

setting, that "this is old Hawaii"? Not ancient Hawaii, granted, but Hawaii before modernization. . . . the way the "real *kama'aina*" remember it.

Scientific Name: Mangifera indica
Family: Anacardiaceae or mango family, 500 species; related to cashews, poison ivy.

Mangoes and dripping, sticky sweetness are inseparable.

Lush lowland vegetation in Hawaii often includes red flowering mango trees.

SEASIDE MORNING GLORY (pohuehue)

Bright purple blossoms typify most of Hawaii's beaches.

Calm and smooth, the sea sparkled under the bright tropical sun. Occasionally a small swell heaved the glassy water up into a gentle wave about six inches high. It was beautiful but no good for surfing.

A party of strapping Hawaiian youths, staggering under the weight of their heavy wooden surfboards, arrived at the beach. They sat down right above high-tide mark, where the seaside morning glories (*pohuehue*) stretched their vine-like runners towards the ocean.

> *"Arise, arise, ye great surfs. . .*
> *The powerful curling waves.*
> *Arise with the pohuehue,*
> *Well up, long raging surf."*

Chanting this intonation, the lads each grabbed several long strands of *pohuehue* and dived into the clear water. They swung the vines around their heads many times, lashing them down forcefully upon the water in unison as they appealed to the gods for help.

Ancient Hawaiian boys loved to surf, and undoubtedly became frustrated, as modern surf-enthusiasts do, when week after week waves failed to assume the perfect height and shape. Perhaps if the above ceremony was performed in a shallow reef area, with enough faith, the gods responded!

Seaside morning glory, today a common beach plant, had particular significance to many Pacific people, including those in Hawaii. Its uses varied tremendously.

Its long stems, which normally criss-cross to form a strong solid mat, were stripped and tied together to form rope hundreds of feet long. In ancient legends, these ropes lowered men from canoes deep down into the underworld of departed spirits. More practically, these vines served as cords in house-construction, for making fishnets and baskets, in medicines, and as famine food. At other times the stems were cut into suitable lengths and slapped onto the breasts of mothers who had just given birth. *Pohuehue*'s milky white sap, with the help of god Ku and goddess Hina, was supposed to stimulate the flow of milk to feed the newborn baby.

Most people are familiar with the typical funnel-shaped flower of a morning glory, with its five-pointed central "star". In the *pohuehue* these flowers are pink or purplish-blue. Although growing under hot dry conditions, they are surprisingly fragile. Pick one and it will droop or become crushed in no time. The old Hawaiians used them in an unusual, rather cute manner. After circumcising a small boy, a *pohuehue* blossom was popped over the end of his penis to promote healing!

The *pohuehue*'s quite leathery leaves possess a characteristic shape too. To me they resemble a butterfly with rounded wings. The scientist who originally named this plant had another idea. He called it *Ipomoea pes-caprae,* which translates to "the vine with leaves like a goat's foot track".

As you walk down almost any Hawaiian beach on a scorching summer's day, your feet smart from the intensely hot sand and your eyes squint from the glare. Isn't it amazing that these (or any shoreline plants really) exist, without wilting, under such conditions?

The *pohuehue* is capable of absorbing water almost as salty as seawater. This requires special chemical processes to eliminate excess salts from the plant's sap. Its leaves, which are not even hairy or succulent, seem not only to withstand the burning sun, but actually thrive on it!

Sand also, for any "normal" plant, is a highly unstable substrate, possessing little nutriment to sustain life. Yet, as *pohuehue*'s roots dig deeply into it, the vine grows rapidly and actually stabilizes large areas of sand, preventing erosion from winds and high waters.

Pohuehue's seeds, enclosed in little woody capsules, are excellent floaters, staying viable after months at sea. Constantly drifting from one island to another, they have reached the farthermost islets in our vast Pacific ocean.

In Hawaii, *pohuehue* luxuriates on most beaches and dunes, especially those on the south coast. Next time you step on these vines, stop a moment to examine it. In addition to its remarkable manner of adapting to a harsh beach environment, it has also managed to survive man's great alterations to our coastline, a rare feat indeed.

Scientific Name: Ipomoea pes-caprae *or I.* brasiliensis
Other names: pohuehue, koali (strictly speaking, these are its dryland relatives)
Family: Morning Glory family or Convulvulaceae; 1,100 species; related to sweet
       potato.

Several species of koali *(*Ipomoea *spp) cheer lowlands and uplands alike.*

K. Kepler

Pohuehue: *a familiar plant to residents and visitors.*

K. Kepler

MOUNTAIN APPLE

('ohi'a-ai)

Springtime blossoms dazzle our eyes – yet they are so ephemeral!

D. Boynton

Pink and white, waxy, apple-sized fruits hang on tiny stalks from the branches and trunks of tall, mountain apple trees. It is quite dim inside the shady, humid grove, but shafts of sunlight streak through the dark foliage, accentuating the luscious appearance of these attractive fruits, each one unique in its combination of crimson, pink and white.

Men living in Pelekunu Valley, Molokai, stretch upwards to pluck fruits or knock them down with long sticks. They gorge on them voraciously. Thin-skinned, with white juicy pulp enclosing a single seed, their flavor is delicate and sweet, reminiscent of a pear . . . a perfect refreshing snack after a long walk on a hot day. (The people of Hawaii had access to very few fruits, thus the late summer months were undoubtedly awaited with great anticipation.)

Besides collecting fruit, the main reason for their hike into this grove is to collect bark from mature trees and tender young leaves from saplings. A woman in their family is about to give birth, and relatives and friends are busy collecting ingredients for various herbal medicines; *kukui* nuts (for oil to massage the baby), *limu* (seaweed to replace lost minerals from the mother's body), *hau* sap (a lubricant), and *pia* (arrowroot starch to be used as "baby powder"). A warmed infusion of mountain apple leaves and bark is an important beverage for the new mother, helping to expel the afterbirth. Even if the baby is aborted, this same tea will be drunk to cleanse the mother's body.

Introduced into Hawaii by early Polynesian settlers, the mountain apple favors the windward areas of our high islands. The name "mountain apple" is a bit of a misnomer, as it is not strictly a mountain tree and is unrelated to apple trees! Like its close relative, the rose-apple, it prefers the lower, humid altitudes and shady valleys. Growing readily among other lowland forest trees such as guava and *kukui*, it may form pure stands, with a ground cover of, for example, shampoo ginger.

Mountain apple trees may be tall and stately, attaining a height of 50 feet. They generally possess straight trunks and are easily recognized by their dark green, glossy, paired leaves and unmistakeable flowers and fruits. Fresh leaves are apple-green, usually tinged with red. Reminiscent of rose-apple or *'ohi'a lehua* flowers, their showy clusters of dark pink, shaving-brush-like blossoms present a dazzling sight in spring and early summer. Borne in great profusion, not at the ends of twigs, as in most fruit trees, but along the length of thick branches, they often peek right out of the smooth-barked trunks fairly low down, like jakfruit. If the grove is dense enough the fallen stamens, which comprise most of the flower, carpet the ground with a richly colored cerise mat.

Formerly mountain apple groves were favorite haunts of native birds, as their blossoms, like *'ohi'a,* secrete sweet nectar. (Incidentally, these trees are botanically related, and were also recognized as kin by the old Hawaiians. Mountain apples were called *'ohi'a-ai.*) Today, because introduced mosquitoes and other factors essentially limit native birds to higher elevations, their songs are rarely heard in these lower mountain slopes. In a few deeply-wooded valleys on Maui and Molokai, where native birds are currently developing a resistance to bird malaria (transmitted by mosquitoes), some of the hardier natives such as the *apapane* are returning to sip nectar from mountain apple flowers.

Sacred to many Polynesians, especially Tahitians, the mountain apple tree (originally from Malaysia) appears to have lost most of its religious association after its arrival in Hawaii. It was an important tree for temple and idol use in Tahiti, where it is called *ahia.* Considering the closeness of the names and appearance of *ahia* and *'ohi'a,* it is very possible that much of this sanctity was transferred to Hawaii's native *'ohi'a* when the first settlers arrived here.

Medicinally its uses were fairly varied, ranging from inducing abortions, aiding childbirth and curing throat and lung complaints. Such treatments primarily utilized pounded bark and leaves. A red dye for patterning tapa (bark-cloth) was extracted from the bark.

If you live in Hawaii's wet lowlands, you can grow your own mountain apple tree from seed. It should grow fast if watered well, bearing in seven or eight years. Late summer and early fall are the times to gather its two-to-three-inch long, pleasant,

Cerise colored stamens blanket the ground by the millions.

K. Kepler

A spray of miniature, pink shaving brushes!

juicy fruits. It is a good idea to attach a mango- or avocado-picker to your car if you collect them from the wild, as the fruits are often tantalizingly beyond reach. They can be eaten raw, or stewed with a little honey, or pickled. In "Fruits of Hawaii" (Miller et al, University of Hawaii Press, 1976) there is a good recipe, or adapt any watermelon rind or sweet pickle recipe.

Another naturalized, Polynesian introduced heritage plant, the mountain apple or *'ohi'a-ai,* for centuries considered a special gift to man from the gods, is a graceful and brilliant addition to our moist forests.

> *"Powers that hold with thee, God Laka (god of agriculture),*
> *He gives the men the rich-ripe mountain apple.*
> *The gods pour out their healing water....."*

from a prayer by Hi'iakà, Pele's sister.

Scientific Name: Eugenia malaccensis
Other names: Mountain apple, Malay apple, Otaheite apple, Pomerac, *'ohi'a-ai*
Family: Myrtaceae or myrtle family, about 2,800 species; related to *'ohi'a lehua,* guava, eucalyptus, allspice, rose-apple, strawberry guava.

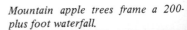

Mountain apple trees frame a 200-plus foot waterfall.

Mountain apple fruits, about 2½ inches long.

BEACH

NAUPAKA

Shiny green leaves, marble-like berries and white half-flowers crawl over hot beach lava.

Naupaka was then born, which stands by the seashore."
from the Kumulipo, Hawaiian creation chant

Many years ago two Hawaiian lovers strolled along a beach, hand in hand. Soon they started an argument and Puna, the girl, in her rage, grabbed a *naupaka* flower (which legend relates was a larger, whole flower in those days) and ripped it in half. She then swore that she would not speak to her boyfriend again until he brought her a new, complete blossom. As soon as she had torn the flower, the gods changed all Hawaii's *naupaka* flowers into half-flowers, the mountain species, as well as the seashore species. Puna's lover searched in vain for a whole flower and eventually died of a broken heart, leaving Puna to regret her emotional outrage. The flowers, many generations later, still grow incompletely.

Many similar stories, attempting to unravel the mystery of the beach *naupaka's* unusual flower, exist in Hawaii's rich folklore. They all involve separated lovers and few, unfortunately, end happily.

On close examination, the whitish, purple-streaked *naupaka* blossom is not a half-flower at all; the flower (about three-quarters of an inch wide) is merely divided by a slit which is so deep that it appears to be missing its top half.

What is the reason for this strange flower? No one really knows, but it seems that the gap between the petals provides a special access route for insects to reach the pollen, in order to effect fertilization.

A sprawling, succulent shrub a few feet high, the *naupaka* has numerous inter-twining branches bearing bunched leaves, white "half-flowers" and clusters of round, white fruits. These lightweight, spongy fruits (*huahekili* or "hailstones" in Hawaiian) originally arrived on our shores after months of tossing in turbulent waves and variable currents.

C. Kepler

Naupaka *adds dimension to Maui's Waianapanapa cliffs.*

A half-flower, typifying the spirit of an unfulfilled lover.

Of Australian affinity, beach *naupaka* is also distributed along sandy, rocky, coralline and lava coastlines all over the Pacific and parts of South-East Asia. It is a friend to many nationalities and races of mankind.

Naupaka are extremely hardy plants. Their remarkable tolerance to sea-water triggered some experiments several years ago. Researchers discovered that *naupaka* seeds, buoyed up by their corky cushioning, *germinated rapidly even after one year of immersion in sea-water!* (That is a better record than a coconut). In addition, the seeds soaked in salt water germinated better than those soaked in fresh water. What a marvellous adaptation for a colonizer of far-flung oceanic shores! Chemical processes within the plant are able to tolerate large amounts of disssolved salts, normally lethal. These salts assist succulence too; if you pick *naupaka* leaves and keep them in fresh water they droop and lose their crispness.

For any plant to succeed in relatively soil-less, windy and salty environments, it needs many adaptations as well as efficient seed-transportation and the ability to germinate in salty water. Special mechanisms enabling beach *naupakas* to survive and thrive as far down as high-tide level include its thick succulent leaves with their generous coatings of wax, and whitish hairs. These characters serve to conserve water and prevent stored water from evaporating too fast. The hairs also reflect sunlight (as any shiny surface does) so that on bright sunny days the plant does not wilt.

Strong, though shallow, root-systems also enable these plants to cling to cliffs, tolerate shifting sand and penetrate pukas in barren lava.

To the ancient Polynesians, beach *naupaka* was not an especially important plant, but it did have occasional uses, especially in emergencies. For example, the initial settlers in Hawaii, familiar with it from islands to the south, ate its insipid, pithy berries, used its bark to aid digestion and whittled its wood into canoe-pegs. *Naupaka* leaves are definitely "famine" food in my opinion!

Look for beach *naupaka* anywhere along Hawaii's coasts, even on beaches adjacent to hotels. It is especially attractive on bare lava outflows, where its vivid green contrasts brilliantly with the black jaggedness of this primordial building substance of our island home.

Scientific Name: Scaevola taccada
Other names: beach naupaka, beach scaevola, *naupaka-kai* ("*naupaka*-by-the-sea"),
　　　naupaka-kahakai ("*naupaka*-along-the-seashore"), *huahekili* ("hailstones")
Family: Goodeniaceae or goodenia family; 250 species; related to lobelias.

Noni: *for centuries a Polynesian cure-all.*

NONI

Furious gusts of wind swirled in every direction around the precipitous cliffs at the mouth of Waikolu Valley, north Molokai. Racing blasts charged down the steep ridges enclosing the bay, while others funneled down the high narrow valley. Circular winds whirled from offshore islands, producing long "rooster tails" on the waves. At times they carried off the tops of the powerful breakers, smashing them against the vertical cliffs. Threatening clouds laden with rain fast approached from the east. Dramatic, yes, but these incessant winds brought another day of misery to the small colony of lepers living out their death sentence in Waikolu Valley. Each had been harshly unloaded offshore with barely a farewell; each had struggled through the turbulent seas to be dumped, bruised, on Waikolu's bouldery strand. Once onshore, each shared in the agony of a living death. Their sole shelters were crudely constructed windbreaks. There was no lumber, no medicine and precious little food.

Noelani, a recent arrival, remembered that her family had used *noni* fruit to cure sores, and was determined to find some. She knew Hawaiians had lived here previously, as she and the other lepers were expected to cultivate and live off taro remaining in the overgrown terraces. Unfortunately they had hardly any driftwood and no sharp tools to procure wood to build a fire to cook it. They were always hungry. Noelani's grandmother had also told her that in emergencies, *noni* could be eaten. In desperation she set off, sloshing through the marshy mud at the stream outlet, and boulder-hopping up the rushing stream. She shivered from the wet cold winds and perpetual dampness, typical of this part of Molokai. Bleating goats echoed above – if only she could capture one! Several spectacular 2,000′ waterfalls bounced down the valley walls, and delicate, pale green maidenhair ferns carpeted rocky embankments, but she was blind to their beauty. Life was hell.

After rounding a bend in the river she spotted a medium-sized tree with large shiny leaves sculptured by prominent veins. A sickly smell of vomitus emanated from the ground below it. Ripe *noni* fruit! With a renewed burst of energy she collected the irregular-shaped, rounded fruits: the hard green ones would serve as passable food, and the soft yellow ones (which made her gag even to pick them up) would make the best medicine.

Back at the shelter, hours later, she rejoined her companions and, for those who welcomed her, she rubbed ripe *noni* juice into their continuously running sores.

They were a motley crew. Several were riddled with the dreaded disease. Bloated faces, vacant eyes, fingerless hands and flaking skin were common symptoms. Many were beyond walking and in constant excruciating pain.

Noni brought hope but was powerless against the ravages of leprosy, a bacterial disease (closely related to TB) with no cure at that time – 1868.

One sunny day Noelani prepared a warm infusion of *noni* juice (using hot beach stones) for a young woman who had recently been raped. They hoped it would initiate a miscarriage, but the woman drowned the next week while trying to catch fish. Law and order were impossible to establish in such an animalistic group. The women were particularly afraid of the men, who at times behaved inhumanly.

Although the above story casts doubt upon the healing powers of *noni,* we need to recall that it was not until 1941 that medical researchers discovered that sulfone drugs could arrest leprosy, and 1946 before these "wonder drugs" arrived in Hawaii. Even today patients need to take the drugs every day for it to be effective, and the side-effects upon kidneys and livers can become quite serious.

The geographical range of *noni* stretches from Africa through Asia into the Pacific. Its Pacific distribution coincides with that of many plants valued by the early Polynesians (such as taro and breadfruit), and clearly marks the eastern and northern migrations of these peoples. *Noni* has long been recognized as an important component of primitive medicine, and is still used in remote places today. Doctors at the University of Hawaii and in the Philippines have isolated its active ingredient, appropriately dubbed "morindin" (from *Morinda, noni's* scientific name).

Richard Marks, a leper now living in Kalaupapa village, Molokai, recalls a rather traumatic event involving *noni* cure. As a boy in Makawao, Maui, he could not hold down any solid food for three weeks. As he was weak and losing weight, his mother took him to a lady herb doctor. After pouring urine on his head (to drive off evil spirits) and chanting loudly, she forced a mixture of ripe *noni* fruit and red peppers down his throat. Cheerfully he jokes that since this dreadful "second-hand vomit" he has always had a hearty appetite! He also recalls when, many years ago, he was scrambling on Molokai's rugged cliffs and toppled into a Christmas berry bush, poking both his eyes. He squeezed *noni* juice into his eyes, bandaged them up, and in a few days they were better.

One can ramble on and on with *noni* stories. Some people prefer ripe fruit, others green. Many drink it as a tonic, others say only to use it externally. It can reputedly cure ailments ranging from arthritis, rheumatism, sores, boils, the vicissitudes of old age, and drive away *uku* (head-lice). In combination with other plants and salt, it has been known to cure broken bones of both horses and people. *Noni* was ineffective against leprosy, undoubtedly man's most abominable affliction. If your children slip and graze their knees though, it might be worth a try, even as a psychological cure for a pair of tiny legs. Many Polynesians still swear by it!

K. Kepler

A spot of beauty in Molokai's Waikolu Valley, an otherwise hellish place for lepers.

Several chiefesses in the village of Hilo, Hawaii needed some yellow dye for their skirts and capes. Only those of royal blood were permitted to wear yellow-dyed tapa (bark cloth), manufactured mostly from *noni,* a plant brought from faraway Tahiti many generations ago. That morning they had sent their servants into the lush lowland forests to gather *noni* roots and fruits.

Later the women sat chatting in the shade as they crushed small sections of *noni* root in stone bowls, using heavy poi-pounders. After separating out the fibrous matter they added the powdered bark to water heating in a large wooden calabash. By periodically adding hot stones from an underground oven they brought this yellow liquid almost to boiling point. When the dye was "cooked" sufficiently they dipped lengths of fresh tapa into it, carefully distributing the folds so their skirts would become colored evenly. Other pieces of tapa were immersed into hot dye to which burnt coral had been added. Lime from this finely ground coral reacted chemically with the yellow *noni* dye to produce red, another exclusively royal shade.

The knowledge of such techniques undoubtedly accompanied *noni* cuttings and seeds as they were distributed over hundreds of years throughout the Pacific. Any book on Polynesian tapa-making describes *noni* as a common, yet special, dye-plant; it was even used into the 20th Century on some islands. In Asia *noni* was also raised commercially for dyes; for example, Indian factories were still operating in 1920.

Noni's curious flower cluster consists of a short stalk bearing many closely packed blossoms in various stages of development – tiny green buds, small white tubular flowers, and the remains of former flowers which have already enlarged into fruits, all closely packed. As the entire cluster continues to mature, several dozen single fruits unite into one large collective fruit similar to the construction of a pineapple or breadfruit. The result is an odd-shaped, warty ball up to five inches in length. *Noni's* large glossy leaves are reminiscent of its relatives, gardenias, whose fruits, incidentally, also yielded a yellow tapa dye.

Noni, found wild today, prefers humid lowland forests along windward coasts. Although the Hawaiians valued *noni* greatly, they never did more than plant a few bushes around their villages. In cultivation it can be found in most botanical gardens or arboratae and around old Hawaiian village sites. A particularly fine old specimen grows in Kalaupapa Village (Molokai) by the gasoline pump.

Of all the plants brought to Hawaii by early settlers, many are not found easily today. Some (such a coconut, banana, *hala* and taro) are common; others (such as *noni* and breadfruit) are less common; and others (such as *'awa, pia, wauke*) are extremely rare. Even though the Hawaiians treasured such plants for food, clothing and medicine, they were not too industrious about cultivating many of them. Where a whole plant was used, people merely yanked it out of the ground, not bothering to replant cuttings or seeds. Consequently useful plants, especially those that required care, gradually disappeared from former abundance. *Noni* did not fare too badly, but if you consider the thousands of plants of paper mulberry (*wauke*) that yielded bark for tapa, it is truly amazing that now only a handful of bushes exist in our entire state of Hawaii! The old Hawaiians could have benefited greatly from a modern course in conservation of natural resources!

One of *noni's* special interests is its specialized seeds. Although they cannot travel long distances at sea, they do possess a woody watertight airsac that enables them to float between closely spaced islands. *Noni's* seeds can survive over a year in salt water and still germinate. On more tropical islands they germinate right along the shore.

Although primarily used medicinally, *noni* fruit was cooked in hard times to make it a bit more palatable. I don't know whether Hawaiians enjoyed its taste; probably not, as it did not form part of their regular diet. Some Pacific islanders, however, relished its foetid taste, eating it even when other foods were plentiful. In the 1920's Niue Islanders ate it regularly, and I have been told that Filipinos made a jam from it, preferring the taste when it was fermented. What a contrast to Richard Marks' description of *noni* fruit as "second hand vomit"! How variable are human food preferences... and how incredibly determined are they by culture.

In addition to the "regular *noni*" that many are familiar with, five native mountain species evolved in Hawaiian forests. Their origin is a mystery; they may have suddenly appeared as mutants from the cultivated *noni* or come via a stray bird.

A source of dye, medicine, wood and famine food, *noni* is a small part of the lingering traces of plant-related culture that dates back thousands of years.

Scientific Name: Morinda citrifolia
Other names: *noni* and its Pacific variations, *nonu, nono,* "wild fig", noni apple, Indian mulberry
Family: Rubiaceae or coffee family, about 5,500 species; related to gardenias, coffee.

Leaves, flowers and fruit of noni.

C. Kepler

Molokai's dramatic north coast, with Waikolu Valley extending to the right.

K. Kepler

Lush, dripping wet lowland forests are favored haunts of noni *plants.*

'OHELO

Halemaumau Crater, Big Island: site of a plant-related historic event.

"Puna spread with fertility, rich in fragrance...
Reddened is the skin of the 'ohelo by the sun,
Sparkling red in the grass is the sacred child;
A reservoir for the running water loosing itself. . ."

from an old Hawaiian chant

Trudging through dense forest and over rough jagged lava, High Chiefess Kapiolani ascended Mauna Loa from sea level to the lip of Kilauea Crater. The year was 1824. Her reason for such an arduous journey, mostly on foot?.... to defy Pele, the famous and powerful Goddess of Fire, and publicly announce faith in her new God, the Christian Jehovah. It was a courageous intention and she carried it out with regal authority.

'Ohelo was a sacred plant; no one could eat of its juicy berries before throwing some into the deep, fiery pit first. *"Pele, here are thy 'ohelo, I offer some to thee; some I also eat"*, was the prayer. Woe betide anyone who disobeyed!

Kapiolani and her followers passed the night in a fern-thatched shelter, and the following morning, amidst the almost overpowering heat, she insulted Pele by hurling stones into the Crater, *and* eating 'ohelo berries without first offering a portion to the Goddess. "Jehovah is my God", she proclaimed. "He kindled these fires. I fear not Pele. If I perish by the anger of Pele, then you may fear the power of Pele; but if I trust in Jehovah, and He shall save me from the wrath of Pele when I break through her *kapu,* then you must fear and serve the Lord Jehovah. All the gods of Hawaii are vain."

Bold statements indeed for her time... Even though five years earlier the old *kapu* (taboo) system had been overthrown, there were still many ardent followers of the old beliefs. It is difficult for us to imagine what a tremendous impact her behavior had on a culture in the midst of a tumultuous religious transition. How could eating a few 'ohelo berries without first offering some to Pele, be proclaimed not only as a spectacular act of bravery but accelerate the spread of Christianity throughout our islands?

But it did. The missionaries used her experience to refute the reality of traditional Hawaiian deities and thus won more converts to the new religion.

Today we have the freedom to munch on as many berries as we wish when visiting Hawaii Volcanoes or Haleakala National Parks, where they are primarily

Tree 'ohelo (Vaccinium calycinum) a close relative of blueberries.

K. Kepler

found. They certainly provide a welcome taste of sweetness and juiciness in these desert-like environments.

'Ohelos are not only good for human consumption; birds, their original carriers, also consume them eagerly. For example, they comprise a good number of the berries eaten by *nene* (Hawaiian geese), our State bird.

Actually, we might as well share them with the birds as in fruiting season (mid-summer to winter) there are always more berries than a large party of thirsty, hungry hikers can consume. The plant's little drooping, bell-shaped flowers, which appear in abundance in spring, ripen to form the familiar colorful, globular berries. Colors range from pale yellow or orange to scarlet. Hikers familiar with high-elevation lava expanses know well that one quickly develops an eye for the berries of a particular size, shape and skin-thickness that are the tastiest, even though they cannot compete with the delicacy and sweetness of blueberries, their relatives.

'Ohelo belongs to a large group of plants well represented in cold mountain areas all over the world; places such as the Rockies, Himalayas, Andes and mountaintops of Pacific Islands. Everywhere they have been distributed by birds. Normally the colder the climate, the better the berries, as anyone who has picked blueberries in Maine will attest. This is why *'ohelo* does not grow in Hawaii's lowlands; it is not a tropical plant at all, but a cold-weather bush that has managed to gain a foothold in the cooler parts of the tropics and subtropics. When I think of the Pacific distribution of *'ohelo*-like plants, my mind automatically visualizes the peaks of its highest islands – Hawaii, Tahiti, Samoa and the Cook Islands. Transferred in bird droppings from mountaintop to mountaintop, such alpine environments really represent "islands" within islands within a vast ocean.

How fortunate we are to live in these times when everyone has almost unlimited freedom! We can not only pick *'ohelo* berries without the overshadowing threat of eternal damnation, but can think and believe as we please. That's pretty unique in the history of mankind!

Scientific Name: Common *'ohelo,* one of six native species, *Vaccinium reticulatum*
Common Name: *'ohelo* ("pink", referring to the rosy berries)
Family: Heath or Ericaceae, about 1500 species; related to heather, cranberries, blueberries, rhododendrons, azaleas.

A tooth-leaved species, the barbery-leaved 'ohelo (V. ber-berifolium), native to alpine scrubland on Maui and Hawaii Is.

C. Kepler

K. Kepler

...hi'a *is primarily responsible for the distinc-*
...e *character of Hawaiian mountain scenery.*
...lalau *Valley, Kauai.*

Twisted gray trunks, rounded foliage and
bright red pompom flowers typify 'ohi'a.

'OHI'A

> *"It is misty above through the clouds, windy is the gap;*
> *Vibrating is the* lehua, *the blossom of the tree;*
> *Cleaving the* 'ohi'a *tree ripe with age..."*

from an old Hawaiian chant

Feathery clouds swirl above Oahu's ridgetops and peaks as a party of Hawaiians trudge up a steep incline overlooking the windward portion of their island. A young lad carelessly plucks a blossom from an *'ohi'a* tree perched precariously on a rocky overhang. The older men chide him, reminding him that *lehua* blossoms are sacred to Pele, the goddess of fire. If she is displeased with his actions she will envelop them with rain, obscuring their path back down the mountain.

After checking out some *'ohi'a* trees for use as temple images, the party returns, though they progress slowly due to sudden stormy weather. The lad is silent and tries to appease Pele's retribution by throwing a scarlet *lehua* lei over the precipice.

Even today some locals hesitate to pick a *lehua* flower when ascending mountains, for fear of rain, and consequently, getting lost.

Since earliest colonization, the *'ohi'a* has figured prominently in the legends and religion of the Hawaiian people. One might suspect that such an abundant tree, occupying almost every type of habitat and providing an excellent hardwood, would be chopped down indiscriminately. But no... *'ohi'a lehua* was a very special tree.

A burst of crimson: sacred to the people of old.

The Hawaiian forests were sacred, and *'ohi'a* in particular, was considered the actual abode of the great and powerful gods of creation, Ku and Kane. Originally no commoner would dare to desecrate a branch or even pick a flower without first obtaining permission from the appropriate gods, goddesses and village chiefs.

How did such reverence originate? Close to the essence and flow of life in a harmonious forest setting, Hawaiians could easily have experienced some every profound feelings. Because *o'hi'a* dominated the mountain verdure, it is natural to assume that people figured that the actual trees were imparting these feelings to them. Over the years they became convinced that the *'ohi'a* tree was the earthly manifestation of the great god Ku.

In those days, *'ohi'a* was primarily used for carving temple images, enclosures, and war-gods (*kukailimoku*). Easy to whittle when fresh, *'ohi'a* was carved only by skilled craftsmen who were well-versed in religious ritual as well as carpentry. The idols were those with ferocious faces that are so familiar today.

By the time Captain Wilkes, of the U.S. Exploring Expedition, arrived in 1845, these elaborate ceremonies involved atrociously unreasonable and barbaric elements. For example, during the construction of King Kamehameha's large *heiau* (temple) at Kohala (Big Island), Wilkes observed an eight-day rite affiliated with *'ohi'a* carving. Many humans, as well as dozens of pigs and chickens, were sacrificed, and prayers, chants and taboos were uttered according to a strict order. At one point, as an *'ohi'a* fell in a certain direction, the chief stripped the owners of their land, grabbed all their belongings and property, then killed them!

It seems pathetic that such savagery evolved from what probably originated as a pure experience of Nature.... an intimate glimpse into the all-pervasive energy of Life itself.

Associated with the sanctity surrounding *'ohi'a* emerges another symbolic association, important in Hawaiian poetry. Love.... a grand love for nature, a binding love for family and friends, and erotic passion too.

One 19th Century poem (composed by Princess Liliuokalani) muses on a man thinking of his sweetheart:

"Entranced with beauty
The lehua *blossoms,*
I come quickly to find
A flower to place upon my heart."

Loving is still symbolized today in the exchange or giving of leis. Up to the 20th Century, scarlet *lehua* leis (often interwoven with ferns and gardenias) were very special leis, especially on the Big Island, where *lehua* is the "island flower."

For many people in contemporary Hawaii, the *'ohi'a* tree barely exists. Symbols of God and love shifted away from nature worship long ago. However, for those who wish to seek it out, much *'ohi'a* forest exists in the remote sections of our mountains, and scattered frees are common along roads, at State Parks and along established trails. We can enjoy hiking amongst its twisted, often moss-covered branches, and watching the native birds that are dependent upon its flowers for food. The less adventurous can admire the plants at any Botanical Garden, snuggle under an old Hawaiian quilt with a *lehua* design, or just sip tea sweetened with *lehua* honey.

Each ties us closer to our native heritage and links us further with the dynamics of Hawaii's living forests.

A rare day dawns high up on Haleakala's moisture-laden windward slopes. The misty rain, normally shrouding this wilderness area, is lifting and dissipating into the

C. Kepler

K. Kepler

plicas of 'ohi'a deities, City of Refuge, Is. Hawaii.

Late afternoon light in a deep, misty gully (6,100').

crystal clear air. Puffy clouds float above the crisp outlines of innumerable ridges and valleys and sunshine highlights the vivid colors of Maui's native forest.

Gnarled, twisted branches of *'ohi'a* trees extend upwards, their pale gray, fissured bark glowing white in the brightness. Irregular gray-green masses of small, close-set leaves typify this attractive tree, so characteristic of our upland vegetation. Its angular trunks, frequently spiralling over great abysses, hide the precipitous nature of this wild country. Gully after gully they clothe, blending with other trees to mingle in a tapestry of natural colors.

A flash of orange-scarlet attracts your eye as a dazzling *'i'iwi,* uttering a flute-like whistle, darts into an *'ohi'a*'s slightly rounded canopy. Its orange curved bill probes deeply into the crimson, shaving-brush-like flowers that dot the uppermost branches.

The *'i'iwi* has joined many other small birds such as the *apapane,* whose red plumage matches the tufted *lehua* pompons perfectly. These songsters contribute to the early moring activity in the tree-tops, uttering a variety of whistling, tinkling and melodious notes. Nectar glands deep inside the *lehua* tassels secrete an abundance of nectar, and all the birds, plus wild bees and other insects, partake of the bountiful supply of energy-packed liquid.

The old Hawaiians could not help but notice this intimate association of forest *'ohi'a* and birds. The bird-catchers were especially knowledgable concerning the habits of the *'i'iwi,* whose feathers were prized for making the famous feathered capes of royalty. These messengers of the chiefs devised many ingenious methods for capturing birds of all sizes.

Originally *'ohi'a* grew almost everywhere in our islands, from the highest peaks almost down to the coast. Understandably it figured prominently in early folklore, such as the following lyrical verse:

'Ohi'a, *a hardy pioneer: 1859 lava flow, Is. of Hawaii.*

C. Kepler

"O honey-dew sipped by the bird,
Distilled from the fragrant lehua...
Scraggly in growth yet scarlet atop
Its nectar wrung out by the birds!"

By the time Captain Cook landed (1778), much of our forested land had been altered extensively and most early visitors did not comment on natural beauty. Hawaiian culture, agricultural methods and political structure kept them sufficiently fascinated. Only the occasional naturalist, willing to devote time and energy to organizing an expedition into the rugged moun-stemming from inclement weather and tough terrain, was rewarded.

Scott Wilson, an old-time ornithologist and a sharp observer, recorded many scientific details relating to *'ohi'a* and its accompanying bird-life. His observations, especially those of now-extinct bird-life, were important in understanding the web of complex interactions between birds and plants within native forests.

Wilson wrote: "These trees are a mass of crimson blossoms and among their branches the *'i'iwi* was in great numbers, busily engaged in probing the flowers in search of nectar... honey will often drip from the bill."

The showy features of the *lehua* flower are not its petals (which are small and rounded), but its numerous long red stamens which comprise the symmetrical tuft. The name *"lehua"* means "hair", and was applied by the Hawaiians to this flower because of the conspicuous hair-like filaments. If you examine the blossom closely, you may notice a resemblance to those of its introduced lowland kin, guavas, rose-apples and mountain apples (see page 94).

The old Hawaiians were most discriminating botanists, having distinctive names for a large proportion of wild plants. For example, they assigned separate names to *'ohi'a* plants with blossoms of different colors (yellow, salmon, wite or red), with leaves of different shapes and degree of hairiness, and with different growth forms.

Each of us enjoys in different ways what we feel to be the "essence" of Hawaii. For those who admire plants, perhaps the coconut palm, hibiscus or plumeria symbolize the beauty of our islands. For me, however, the *'ohi'a lehua,* with its twisted trunks and gay pompon blossoms, is the ultimate expression of our beautiful islands. Accompanied by a rich understory of shrubs and lacy ferns, the upland *'ohi'a* forests dominate our craggy mountains and steeply-eroded valleys, producing a landscape that is truly Hawaiian... a special place where one may encounter anew the miracles of Life and Love.

Scientific Names: *Metrosideros collina polymorpha* ("heart of iron with many forms")
Other names: *'ohi'a lehua, 'ohi'a, lehua* (strictly its flower)
Family: Myrtle or Myrtaceae, about 2,800 species; related to Eucalyptus, guava, rose-apple, mountain apple, Java Plum, paper bark, strawberry guava.

A bird's eye view of 'ohi'a forest. Koolau
gap, Maui.

C. Kepler

Clouds, sun, rainbows... daily transients in
Hawaii's upland forests.

K. Kepler

D. Boynton

An 'i'iwi probes for his staple food of 'ohi'a nectar. What dazzling colors!

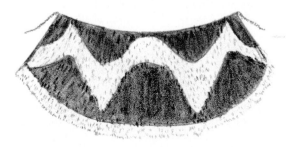

Hawaiian feather cloak with 'i'iwi feathers.

K. Kepler

An unusually large thicket of oloná, *source of ancient ropes, string and threads.*

Oloná: *globular flowers and large, translucent leaves.*

OLONÁ

The summer has been dry and streams in the numerous valleys of East Molokai are low. A few Hawaiian men are scrambling up a small watercourse towards a relatively flat area where their chief's *oloná* patch is located. Twelve moons ago they planted their last crop, extending the previous clearing, chopping down trees and hacking at the luxurious undergrowth with stone adzes. It was tough work. They left some large trees to provide shade, then inserted hundreds of cuttings into the ground. Older plants were pruned to allow for fresh growth. For weeks the men returned to rip out strangling morning glory vines.

Now, months later, they are anxious to see if their valuable fiber crop has grown to perfection. As they round the bend and climb a small waterfall, they happily spy them: large-leaved nettles four to eight feet high, in a dense uniform stand, their straight stems nearly two fingers wide. Some grow right in the streambed.

Joyfully they return to Halawa village and prepare to bring women and children to the mountains to help harvest the *oloná*. The chief, naturally, is immediately informed of his potential wealth.

Back at the *oloná* patch people construct rude shelters and begin cutting long shoots (six feet long by one inch wide), Carefully they strip the bark off with *opihi* (limpet) shells, then weight it down in a shallow placid section of the stream to soak for a day or two. After soaking, the remaining wet pulp is scraped off. Men and women work fast and skillfully. Turtle shell scrapers fly back and forth over long narrow, hardwood anvils, separating out the strong, fine fibers. The most adroit workers complete several hundred barkstrips each day, work which includes rolling fibers for transportation back to the village. There they are sun-bleached to increase their whiteness and are twisted into various thicknesses of attractive, white cordage.

In the late 19th Century Samual Kamakau noted: "When one went into an *olonà* scraping shed, the *olonà* would be seen streaming down like waterfalls over the cliffs, white as the snows of Mauna Kea, 'Fluffy' as curly hair."

Think for a moment about stone-age cultures. Strong ropes and string were immensely important in a world without nails, cotton thread, nylon, catgut, hemp, reinforced tape or man-created fibers. Nature can be exceedingly kind to primitive people in providing essentials for living. In *olonà* the resourceful Hawaiians struck a bonanza! Modern strength tests by the U.S. National Bureau of Standards have shown that *olonà*, Hawaii's endemic fiber plant, possesses strengthened inner bark filaments superior to any other known natural fiber in the world. For example, *olonà* is eight times stronger than hemp!

Before contact with white man, *olonà* was venerated as a lesser deity. Prior to spinning, men and women sacrificed hogs, chickens or fish, and chanted *mele* (prayer songs) such as the following one, which describes vividly the preparation of a fish-net:

> *"I, as chief, willingly cast my net of* olonà;
> *The* olonà *springs up, it grows, it branches and is cut down.*
> *Stripped is the bark of the* olonà, *peeled is the bark. . .*
> *The fire exhales a sweet odor; the sacrifice is ready.*
> *The bark is peeled, the board is made ready,*
> *The* olonà *is carded and laid on the board.*
> *White is the cord. The cord is twisted on the thigh,*
> *Finished is the net! Cast it into the sea. . ."*

Windward Maui and east Molokai were the principal areas in which *olonà* was grown, although evidently every chief had his patch in the wet mountains, tended by commoners. Although these wild plants were cared for in a semi-cultivated manner, they were never abundant. Akin to gold in other cultures, *olonà* indicated a chief's wealth, was always in demand, and consistently demanded a high price.

Early traders avidly bartered for its thick ropes; one sea-captain claimed that *olonà* was stronger than his ropes of twice the diameter, and several others replaced their entire ship's rigging. It was also much sought after by whalers for harpoon lines.

On the Big Island, as late as the 1870's, King Kalakaua required that taxes be paid in *olonà*, which he sold at high prices to Swiss Alpine Clubs, who valued it for its extraordinary light weight and high tensile strength. It also does not kink (as does coconut sennit), nor soak up much water, and is relatively "soft" even in the thickest guages. These properties were important to European mountain hikers, Hawaiian fishermen and New England whalers alike. Even further, *olonà* cord looks lovely: it is so pliable that fibers correctly spun present so uniform a caliber and twist they appear to be machine-made.

Additionally, it possesses a remarkable resistance to salt water deterioration. Almost all Hawaiian fishing gear was manufactured from it. Tanning with natural bark infusions (such as *kukui*) prolonged its life further, and there are records of fishnets and lines which, after 50 years of constant use, were still in excellent condition! Even in the early 20th Century natives were reticent to part with *oloná* fishing paraphernalia, which ranged from stout nets capable of trapping large turtles and man-eating sharks, to those "almost as fine as a spider-web", designed for capturing tiny baitfish.

Delicate "woven" backings for feathers cloaks (the Hawaiians had no true weaving); threads for stitching tapa into garments and tying off babies' umbilical cords; stout cords attached to weapons and stone adzes; canoe lines and lei threads were a few of the numerous uses to which this versatile fiber was put.

A member of the nettle family, *oloná* is unusual in that neither it, nor any of its Hawaiian relatives, possess stinging hairs. In other countries, where large native mammals munch eagerly on vegetation, people normally despise nettles and their protective armor. But not in our remote Polynesian outpost! Why should a plant have spines if nothing is going to eat it up?

A striking plant with large serrated leaves (up to 14 inches long and with three prominent veins) and clustered, orange, mulberry-like fruits, it is quite uncommon today, but not rare. It prefers to grow between about 800' and 1800' elevation in well-shaded, wet locations. When hiking in deep mountain gullies one occasionally runs across a few plants, usually associated with bananas, wild taro or other nettles, It is very difficult to cultivate and is not in any botanical or private garden as far as I know.

A few people still collect *oloná* and twist small quantities of cordage. Two of these are the vivacious Oahu ladies, Beatrice Krauss and Veronica Medeiros, who periodically give demonstrations or teach at the Lyon Arboretum on Oahu. They might use bobby pins to separate the fibers instead of the traditional shell scraper, but then, times *have* changed!

Much is spoken of fishing canoes and tapa, and their importance to the ancient Hawaiian culture. But what is the use of fishing if you don't have reliable nets and lines, and of what use is tapa without any thread to sew it into garments?

Scientific Name: Touchardia latifolia
Family: Nettle or Urticaceae, about 480 species; related to stinging nettles, *mamaki.*

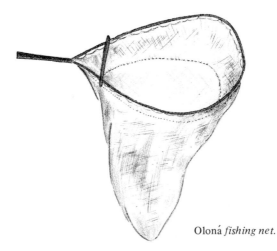

Oloná *fishing net.*

PUAKALA
(Hawaiian
poppy)

Hawaii's spiniest plant, an ancient source of painkillers.

The girl's whole face hurt. Her throbbing toothache had made her miserable for days and she was now writhing in pain. Her friends hurried to provide relief for her unrelenting torment. Their village at Wekea, located on Maui's dry southern slopes near Kaupo, was conveniently close to many wild prickly Hawaiian poppy plants. Soon her friends were collecting the plants, scraping their stems, then pounding and heating the yellowish sap with some of its oily seeds. This mixture they applied to the girl's affected gums and teeth. Miraculously her suffering ceased, and later the infected tooth was extracted painlessly by a *kahuna lapa'au* (medicine man).

The Hawaiians were not the only people to recognize the anaesthetic properties of their local poppies. The more well-known opium poppy, cultivated in Europe and Asia for nearly 2000 years, has also cured many a tooth- and back-ache with its gummy sap scraped from ripening seed-pods. The little that we know concerning the Hawaiian's poppy indicates that at least three narcotic agents (including morphine) are present, although in much lower quantities than in the opium poppy. *Puakala* was used either as crushed stems or grated roots; both preparations were extremely distasteful. It was important to administer correct quantities also, as modern research has uncovered poisonous properties. This is perhaps why our Hawaiian poppy was only used for pain-killing and sedation — never as a psychotic drug. In addition to toothache, it alleviated a variety of serious pains and helped cure ulcers.

What a godsend such a narcotic must have been to the people of old! Reading some of the early missionary journals enables us to gain insight into the tremendous sufferings and agonizing deaths that early Hawaiians experienced. Many of us have, at times, felt the urge to steer away from the mainstream of modern civilization. However attractive the virtues of a simple, isolated life may be, they fade into insignificance as we recall those moments of intense pain, whether it be an infected tooth or a ruptured appendix, when we greatly appreciated the blessings of modern medical technology!

Puakala, peculiar to Hawaii, is a very prickly plant, reaching four feet high, with striking white flowers. It is immediately recognizable as a relative of ornamental poppies. It was first noted by Captain Cook in 1778, and today grows in dry rocky soils, wastelands or pastures form sea-level to about 2000' elevation. Unlike many roadside plants, it does not invite you to pick its fragile, thin-petalled blossoms, which incidentally, wilt immediately anyway. The whole plant is armed generously with skin-piercing spines which cover its crinkled, holly-like leaves,

K. Kepler

Hawaiian poppies thrive in dry wastelands.

flowerbuds, stems and seed-capsules. (In this respect, a parallel situation to *akala,* Hawaii's native raspberry, also prickly in some areas, has arisen.) *Puakala's* closest relatives are also mainland species which developed sharp defenses to prevent being eaten up by mammals. Since arriving in Hawaii, land lacking in native browsers, these plants have not had enough geological time to lose their spines. Botanists tell us that *puakala* arrived very recently, not long before Polynesian man, barely 1500 years ago. If it had arrived many thousands or millions of years ago, we would probably be seeing a spineless poppy bush today. It could well have lost its narcotizing properties too.

The Hawaiians told a riddle concerning their spiny plants (*kala* = spiny):
The kala of the uplands (*akala* berry),
The kala in-between (*puakala* poppy),
The kala of the sea (*limu kala* or Sargassum weed).

Plants are remarkable at adapting themselves to wet or dry living conditions. Many dryland bushes are grayish-white (such as the silversword), due to a dense covering of white hairs on their leaves and stems. The *puakala* is white too, but instead of having hairs, it is covered with a protective coating of white wax, which is another means of accomplishing precious water conservation.

Puakala's seeds possess a wonderful capacity for germinating freely, even under drought conditions or after ravaging fires. Such seed-vitality is essential for survival in arid regions with irregular rainfall.

This interesting poppy also claims another distinction: it is one of Hawaii's few native plants that is not a perennial (that is, living many years). Research in tropical climates indicates that long-established plants tend to become biennials (living two years) and later, perennials. As Hawaii's climate has no great extremes of temperature as in temperate regions, there is no necessity for plants to die back each year. Many visitors are amazed at how our vegetation grows all-year, although to us it is no surprise. A "newcomer" to our islands, *puakala* is a biennial; it has not quite made that last step towards becoming a perpetually growing perennial, as have almost all our other native plants.

To some, *puakala* may be an undesirable spiny weed, but it possesses a beautiful delicate flower, and in olden times was certainly an invaluable addition to Hawaiian pharmacology.

Scientific Name: Argemone glauca ("The whitish poppy that cures white eye-spots")
Other names: puakala ("spiny flower"), Hawaiian or prickly poppy, *kala*
Family: Papaveraceae or poppy family, about 850 species; related to other poppies.

C. Kepler

Inhabitants of this Hawaiian site undoubtedly sought after puakala *many years ago.*

Yellow-fruited akala *berries, another native* "kala" *(spiny) plant.*

K. Kepler

Large native raspberry flowers mature into fruits one inch in diameter, but don't touch akala's *stems!*

K. Kepler

K. Kepler

Dwarfed pukiawe *and* 'ohi'a, *only a few inches high in soggy bogs such as this.*

High elevation pukiawe *scrub on Haleakala, Maui, 8000'. Note the Island of Hawaii in the distance.*

PUKIAWE

Whistling merrily as his mule ambles down the steep switchback trail leading into Haleakala Crater, Joe Medeiros, a former State biologist, is brimming with joy. Behind him are more mules, loaded with gear, and Boy Scouts carrying *nene* (Hawaiian geese) in cardboard packs strapped to their backs. All are headed for Paliku, a green oasis ten miles distant across hot, barren cinders and sparsely vegetated lava desert. The date is June, 1962.

Most of the birds have flown (aboard an airplane) 9000 miles from England to Maui, with stopovers in New Jersey and Honolulu for quarantine. They are the first captive-bred *nene* to be released into the wild after 13 years of intensive work to save them from extinction. Absent from Maui for decades, *nene* are now to be set free in Haleakala's vast, multicolored, volcanic caldera... free to fly up the ridges and into the mists, just as their ancestors did for thousands of years. What an exciting day!

Tired and sweating, the party arrives at the head of Kaupo Gap in the late afternoon. Ah... that cool water tastes wonderful! It's been a sweltering day. Large pens of steel posts and wire, enclosing many types of grasses and wild berries such as *pukiawe* and *'ohelo,* are awaiting occupancy. Each bird is examined, banded, wing-clipped and placed in the pen, where it runs around, pecking eagerly at tender grass shoots. Somehow it knows that the wild berries are good to eat, even though it has been reared on "prepared food".

C. Kepler

Nene: *Hawaii's State bird and a lover of* pukiawe *berries.*

Within two months these captive *nene* will regrow their flight feathers and venture from their open-topped pens into "greener pastures", to be nourished further by the crater's wild berries. Next winter they will breed on their own.

In the early 19th Century, days of *nene* abundance (when an estimated 25,000 birds inhabited Maui and the Big Island), naturalists such as Andrew Bloxam were quick to note the *nene*'s prediliction for *pukiawe* berries: "... wild geese frequent this part of the country and live on the purple berries". From recent, astonishing findings of subfossil bird bones in lava tubes and sand dunes, we now know that there were at least nine other species of large geese, all bigger than *nene*, and all flightless, which inhabited the upper mountain slopes of our major islands. Perhaps they too were dependent on *pukiawe* berries for survival. Whatever they ate, it made their flesh very tasty, hence their extinction by hungry Hawaiians before Captain Cook arrived.

A common, small shrub found abundantly at higher elevations (especially on Maui and the Big Island), *pukiawe* is most evident by its pink, rose or white berries, which always seem to be on the plant. Formerly used for leis, these ¼" diameter fruits are today an important source of food not only for *nene* but for introduced game-birds such as Ring-necked Pheasants. Most abundant in winter, they are not poisonous, as some believe, but neither are they juicy or tasty. I'd take an *'ohelo* any day!

Pukiawe belongs to a relatively small family found primarily in Australia and New Zealand, but its adapations to high altitude "desert" conditions parallel those found in many plants from widely-differing families. This is because temperature extremes, low precipitation and other environmental factors dictate how a plant must be if it is to survive.

Pukiawe's leaves, for instance, are small, narrow and flattened, possessing such leathery surfaces that they are quite prickly. Their tight, spiral arrangement and lack of leaf-stalks ensure that no precious water is lost unnecessarily from their tissues. They are unpalatable to grazers, for obvious reasons, although goats and pheasants will nibble at these sharp-pointed leaves if absolutely nothing else is available. In some areas of Haleakala Crater, where goat concentration is high, *pukiawe* bushes have been pruned up to the highest level that goats can stretch on tip-toes, resulting in mushroom-shaped bushes.

Pukiawe's tiny, star-like flowers appear in abundance during spring. A faint cinnamon odor emanates from the bushes in full bloom, which attract the eye with their contrasting colors of light and dark green foliage mingling with the white flowers and bright pink berries. (Alpine plants usually produce small white or yellow flowers, because such blossoms are usually pollinated by wind or color-blind insects.) The overall shape of *pukiawe* is also characteristic of alpine vegetation: low, rounded and woody. Wind speed increases with distance from the ground, so it is advantageous for high altitude plants to stay short. If the bush is exposed, the wind will prune and stunt it anyway.

Pukiawe must have arrived in Hawaii early in our plant history, undoubtedly brought by a stray bird from the south-west Pacific. After adapting to the dry, cindery regions, it moved into other habitats, becoming a real "generalist". Today, ranging from sea level to almost 10,000', it thrives in the hottest, wettest, driest and coldest regions of our islands. In drippy rainforests and protected valleys it has become a lanky tree with softer, less prickly leaves. Tiny plants even seem to thrive as miniature bonsais, three inches high, in water-saturated bogs, proudly bearing a single berry beside an *'ohi'a* tree of equal size bearing a single scarlet pompon!

Perhaps this remarkable ability to adapt to any amount of sun and rain was why the Hawaiians held *pukiawe* in high esteem. Its most important use was one that is

Haleakala Crater, Maui, a very special home for both pukiawe *shrubs and* nene *geese.*

K. Kepler

entirely unnessary today! Smoke from its burning wood was psychologically able to temporarily lift the dreaded *kapu* (taboo) from a chief. By enclosing himself in a small hut and allowing *pukiawe* smoke to pervade his skin and clothing, then reciting a "dispensation prayer", a chief could then socialize with common people without bringing either harm. Why this same wood was also used for cremating criminals is a mystery to me!

May the haunting cry of our State bird, returned from near-extinction, fill our souls anew with that special, primaeval wilderness feeling of wild birds in wild places, and may we acknowledge our debt to the *pukiawe* berries that helped them survive.

Scientific Name: **Styphelia Tameiameiae** (named after Kamehameha the Great)
Other names: pukeawe, pikiawe, puakeawe, maiele, kawa'u, 'a'ali'i-mahu
Family: Australian Heather or Epacridaceae; its closest relative is in Tahiti; the family is related to true heathers, and *'ohelo* and blueberries.

'ene pens at Paliku Cabin, site of many nene *transplants from captivity in efforts to prevent*
—eir extinction.

C. Kepler

*Colorful, four-petalled flowers of sandalwood (*Santalum haleakalae*).*

*Another species of native sandalwood (*Santalum freycinetianum), *chopped down mercilessly in the "Sandalwood Era".*

SANDALWOOD
('ili-ahi)

Sandalwood: the name reeks of culture. It is one of the few English words derived from ancient Sanskrit.

Images of Asia dance before our eyes. Tranquil Buddhas sitting motionless while burning incense wafts around them; Chinese artisans carving boxes of intricately inlaid woods; well-to-do Brahmins dotting colorful sandalwood paste on their faces to distinguish their caste; colorful bazaars offering sandalwood trinkets for sale. In Hawaii we recall thousands of natives toiling in our rugged mountains, heavy logs strapped to their bare backs, and recollect the ruinously wasteful, newly acquired opulence of Hawaii's royalty.

From the remotest times in history sandalwood, a precious resource, has been coveted in Asia. It is even mentioned in India's oldest scriptures, the Vedas, which date back many thousands of years. Unlike most popular trees, it was not prized for its dimensions, showy grain or ornamental flowers. It was its inner core that mattered. This heartwood has a marvellous cedar-like scent produced by an aromatic oil that permeates its tissues. Once cut, the wood will exude this pleasant odor for up to 60 years. Sandalwood was (and still is) carved into fine household ornaments, incense holders and other religious items. Oils, pressed and distilled from sandalwood seeds and heartwood, are used in cosmetics, medicines, perfumes and lubricants for massaging.

A worldwide human trait is the demand by royal or wealthy people for the finest items to place in their temples, palaces and homes. The acquisition of such luxuries usually requires great expense and effort, and the special items in great demand are often those in limited supply. Even millenia ago, such desires had a tremendous impact on the environment. For example, man's "Cradle of Civilization", the Near East, today a desert, was originally covered with vast forests, some of them sandalwood.

In order to build his opulent House of the Lord, and also a palace for himself, wealthy King Solomon purchased immense amounts of virtually every valued material known at the time, including sandalwood, cedar, gold, silver, ivory and precious stones. After his "fourscore thousand hewers" (80,000) had worked for several years in Lebanon, the Bible tells us that "there came no such *almug* (sandalwood) trees, nor were seen unto this day". So we can assume that the reason the King then sent his woodchoppers and ships to India for more sandalwood, was that he wiped out Lebanon's supply! (He also practically exterminated the famed cedars of Lebanon.) Thus it appears that this revered king must have been the first of the ruthless exploiters of the world's sandalwood forests, heralding an immensely important period for Hawaii almost three thousand years later.

India's sandalwood forests must have been vast, as they were felled for centuries. Her sandalwood is recognized as the best in the world. Given the material poverty of India today, we forget that up until the 18th Century it was one of the wealthiest nations on earth. Knowledge of her priceless treasures were well known in the Orient and later spread to Europe as well. Explorers such as Marco Polo returned to their homelands with remarkable tales of sandalwood and teak, glittering jewels, fancy brocades, gorgeous flowers, colorful birds and cure-all medicines, beginning a long period of intensive exploitation. Over the years, supplies of these treasures dwindled as greater and greater demands were placed upon them.

India's sandalwood supply was rapidly diminishing by the time Captain Cook discovered Hawaii (1778). Within a short time word spread that a similarly fragrant wood abounded on these forested islands. Thus the stage was set for Hawaii's entry into the world of commerce. India's sandalwood supply was low, its prices exhorbitant in Oriental and European markets, shipping routes across oceans were reasonably well charted, and because of a long tradition of demand for the wood, steady business was assured. The wily traders must have been overjoyed to realize that the Hawaiians had not been exposed to Western civilization long enough to have any clues about "real business".

The next chapter in this unfolding drama touches on what I feel was the most unfortunate and heart-rending period of Hawaii's history, an era that decimated villages and forests, jerking our islands into the international world of trade and politics and shaping our future destiny.

The "Lady Washington" had just left Kauai. Her captain, John Kendrick, was a pioneer fur-trader. His route had taken him from Boston to the north-west coast of America to pick up seal and sea-otter furs, then to the Sandwich Islands (as Hawaii was then known) for water, wood and salt. He was on his way to China to sell his goods before sailing back to Boston.

He had purchased some firewood on Kauai, and as the meal cooked, the pleasant odor emanating from the fire excited him. Was this the famous sandalwood of the Far East? If so... his mind started reel. He knew all the lucrative articles of com-

"New Hazard" of Salem, Massachussetts, a typical sandalwood trading vessel.

merce and their current prices, and he was also aware that the price of sandalwood at that time (1790) was escalating rapidly because India's supply was low. And, even more importantly, he realized that his livelihood, fur-trading, was in jeopardy as almost all the seals and otters had been killed. Aha... he had it! He would become a rich man, Hawaii's first sandalwood merchant!

Details of the first 15 years of Hawaii's sandalwood trade are sparce. We assume that Kendrick devoted himself to this lucrative venture because the next record of him is his death in Honolulu four years later. By 1810 this new trade was flourishing. Enormous monetary gains were amassed by traders as they traveled back and forth from Hawaii to the busy harbors of the Orient. Cleverly they wheeled and dealed with the Hawaiian chiefs and kings, who at first had no understanding of commercial values. How could we expect them to? These people were isolated Polynesians with completely different value systems, beliefs and ways of life. They had only a few years earlier seen their first white man.

To make matters worse, the Hawaiian chiefs could not understand why these pale-faced foreigners became so excited about sandalwood, as it did not mean much to them. Why, these haoles would give practically anything for a load of wood easily procured from the mountains!

Although various species of sandalwood occur naturally in forests from Indo-malaya and Australia all across the Pacific, the tree was not culturally important anywhere. Wherever it occured, however, its aroma was known and utilized in ways in which it could be appreciated. Certainly the traditions associated with it did not come close to the sanctity attributed to it in Asia, where it was a precious "jewel", intimately tied to religion, wealth and royalty.

The ancient Hawaiians had named it " 'la'au-'ala" (sweet wood) as well as 'ili-ahi (which referred to the red color of new leaves or the overall redness of flowering trees). They used it mostly for scenting their tapa (bark cloth). By pounding chips from its heartwood into *wauke* bark as they made tapa, the fragrance would remain in their clothes for years. More often they layered wood slivers between folds of tapa during storage. Occasionally they also added sandalwood chips to coconut oil, then used this mixture for waterproofing tapa.

On other Pacific islands, such as Tonga, the technique of retaining sandalwood's scent was more refined than in Hawaii. Natives powdered the heartwood using the sandpapery skin of stingrays as a grater, then mixed these fine particles with coconut oil. Girls rubbed this into their skin after bathing. They must have been irresistible!

Shrewd and often unethical, these white traders deceived the Hawaiians for as long as they could, i.e. until the sandalwood supply ran out. They dangled enticing "carrots" before the wide eyes of chiefs and kings. At first a bunch of old army uniforms, some liquor, muskets or European tophats sufficed for an entire shipload of sandalwood. Later the king's tastes improved, as Chinese silks and embroideries, Morocco leather and the like, were offered. Whatever they saw they wanted and

Boat hull measuring template for sandalwood loads, Molokai.

bought, regardless of price. Recklessly they paid ridiculous sums with sandalwood as currency. One mirror was purchased for $800 and a brass cannon for $10,000! For years, with the consent of eager, competing traders, whole shiploads of extravagant purchases were accepted on credit for sandalwood to be delivered later. Royal debts mounted alarmingly and the poor commoners were packed off to the mountains to gather every precious scrap of wood in sight.

What a disaster, not only financially, but socially as well. Hawaii's forests, at the elevations at which sandalwood grew, never recovered.

Meanwhile, in Asia, where Hawaii was known as "Tahn Heung Shan", the Sandalwood Mountains, most of the prized wood burned slowly away in the temples......

It was July, 1822, Waialua Bay, Hawaii. The bay was alive with activity. Men, women and children were moving back and forth carrying loads of sandalwood logs from a large storehouse down to the beach. A rich, powerful and tyrannical chief, Ke'eaumoku and his attendants were supervising the operations, and the captain of an American ship, for whom the cargo was destined, checked the weighing operations and made sure of safe delivery to his vessel.

From many miles away, far into the mountains on Keeaumoku's land, 2,000 to 3,000 people threaded their way down to the bay where the sailing ship lay at 'anchor. Scenes such as this were common. Chiefs like Ke'eaumoku were merciless in their demands upon the native people. Whole families were sent into the mountains for days, sometimes weeks at a time, eating little except dried poi and wild bananas. No one was permitted to return to his village until he had cut, debarked, and carried certain quantities of sandalwood heartwood to his imperious chief.

There were no beasts of burden in those days, so everything was transported on bare backs. Heavy sandalwood logs up to eight feet long and 1½ feet in diameter were hauled by men, women and children. They were tied to them by *ti*-leaf bands passed across the shoulders, under their arms, and fastened across their chests. Shoulder callouses were so obvious on so many people that traders called Hawaiians *kua-leho,* the "callous backs".

It is no wonder that the poor people's backs were strained! Sandalwood was sold and priced by the "picul", which equalled 133 1/3 lbs, the amount of wood that each man was supposed to carry on each trip from the mountains! (During the Sandalwood Era, the price per picul in Canton ranged from $8 to $10, dropping to $1.50 at the end when the quality was poor). It has been said that every piece of sandalwood cut during those boom years was stained with blood. Some villagers died in harness, crumbling motionless on the trails; others, less fortunate, turned into living skeletons, weak from the corroding effects of exhaustion, disease, malnutrition, and exposure to the chilly mountain winds without adequate clothing. To aggravate matters, much cutting was done at night with the aid of sandalwood torches.

Some of the narrow mountain trails along the sides of precipitous cliffs and deeply cleft valleys (for example, Waipio on the Big Island) were said to be hardly passable in places even to an unencumbered person. Undoubtedly people toppled over the bluffs with no-one to record the events.

Other punishments were inflicted upon the poor commoners. Chiefs such as Ke'eaumoku were so greedy for sandalwood that they readily burned homes and confiscated people's land, wives and children if they refused to obey orders. Chiefs fought for the possession of more property, and others insisted that natives not only pick up every stick but dig roots as well (roots were only 20% less valuable than the tree itself). Naturally no measures were taken to replace trees or protect new growth, or even allow trees to resprout from stumps.

At least two major famines occurred in Hawaii during the Sandalwood Era; many villages were on the verge of starvation because farming was neglected. It marked the beginning of an agricultural decline in Hawaii and a greater dependence on imported goods, a legacy which remains today.

In time, shipments decreased as the quality of wood, and thus its price, diminished. By the early 1830's the government finally decided to conserve the resource. By then it was too late.

While it lasted, sandalwood was a bonanza to the adventurous, canny traders. Although the kings and chiefs were amply rewarded with material goods and power, their subjects suffered horribly. During a period of about 25 years, the trade brought an estimated $3 or $4 million worth of goods (mostly unnecessary luxuries and alcohol) into Hawaii. What a detrimental price to pay for the tremendous loss of precious lives, the pain and hardship, the decline in island self-sufficiency, and the irreparable damage to our forests!

––––––––––

"Hawaiian Sandalwood", the famous 19th Century export, comprised at least three species. All fragrant, they were taken primarily from Oahu, the Big Island, and Kauai. Molokai is rarely mentioned in early accounts, but an interesting momento of that era is preserved on the road to Waikolu Lookout. This is a large depression, now in mown grass, having the same dimensions as a ship's hull (see photo on page 125). When such a sandalwood pit (*lua moku 'ili-ahi*) was filled with logs, the "cargo" was complete and would be carried miles down the mountain to the waiting vessel. Molokai's logging operations must have been very thorough, as few sandalwood trees are left now.

The greatest concentrations of the trees, at least on Oahu, grew from 300' to 1000' elevation in drier forests. Others, less abundant, occurred up to 4000'. Despite decimation of these forests in the early 19th Century, later cutting by settlers, forest recession, and cattle grazing, sandalwood is fortunately not extinct, but still survives in the more inaccessible areas of Oahu's Forest Reserves. Thank goodness for rugged topography! The majority of the remaining trees measure less than 18" in diameter. Because of their painfully slow growth, Dr. Harold St. John (Bishop Museum) considers that they are practically all leftovers from about 1830. The few larger trees, such as one 65' high, may well be ones which escaped the axe 150-odd years ago.

Sandalwoods are unusual in that they require the presence of certain other plants; they have the habit of "stealing" part of their food from them. Our local species will use just about any plant as a host: *koa*, bushes such a *pukiawe*, grasses and even introduced weeds. Without this nutritive help they rarely survive a year.

Sandalwood in full bloom – a riot of color.

While still small, a seedling sends out long roots whose specialized sucking organs attach to the roots of other plants, extracting food from them. Thus sandalwood is a "root parasite". As a result of this, sandalwoods have lost some of their food-manufacturing chlorophyll, and their leathery leaves tend to be blue-green instead of bright green. Flower clusters in Hawaii come in two shades: red and bright green, while their fruits look a bit like little olives with caps on.

Sandalwood is an integral part of Hawaii's historical heritage. If you are interested in seeing these trees, here are a few suggestions: Lyon and Waimea Arboretae (Oahu), Iliau Nature Loop, Waimea Canyon (Kauai), and, on Maui, Haleakala National Park and the Botanical Garden at the Zoo.

The story associated with it continued a tradition begun with King Solomon, who probably exterminated Lebanon's sandalwood and cedar forests centuries ago. When India's supply also declined, Hawaii and other Pacific islands (especially Fiji) were also exploited to exhaustion, simultaneously bringing much sorrow and bloodshed to their people. Foresters have made great advances in propagating Indian sandalwood, which is today grown in large plantations. Because of various known and unknown factors, sandalwood has not done well commercially in Hawaii. (If it ever does, it would be a lucrative business, as a six by two-inch piece of heartwood sells today in India for $20, and about ten times that in New York!)

There are no untouched natural sandalwood forests left in the world. Actually, the percentage of the earth's surface left in natural forests is alarmingly small, decreasing every day. Some countries have far-sighted forestry programs, so we will always have some types of wood such as pine. Also the world's supplies of precious resources — gold, copper, coal and oil can never be replaced; we will continue to exploit them rapidly, like the sandalwood merchants did, until there are none left.

Aldous Huxley once aptly commented: "The greatest lesson in history is that man never learns from history."

Scientific Name: Santalum species
Other names: 'ili-ahi, 'la'au-'ala, 'la'au-'a'ala
Family: Santalaceae or sandalwood; about 400 species.

K. Kepler

Badly chewed up by goats and later eroded by water, this steep country today harbors only occasional sandalwood trees.

Lone sandalwood tree in a pasture: reminder of former days.

A coastal and foothill sandalwood (S. ellipticum) with less aromatic heartwood than other species.

K. Kepler

K. Kepler

Silversword's daisy ancestors are unmistakable here.

Inside a rosette: what design could be more perfect?

SILVERSWORD

"Oh, what beauty! What sublimity! What wonder! Brighter and brighter grew the horizon, until first a tint, then a setting of gold on every undulating eastern gaunt, desolate abyss, with its fiery cones, its rivers of black, surging lava, and gray ash crossing and mingling all over the area, mixed with splotches of color and coils of satin rock. Its walls, dark and frowning, everywhere riven and splintered, with clouds perpetually drifting in through the great gaps like armies of ghosts in silent review, filling up the whole crater with white swirling masses... rainbows and sunkissed clouds (were) everywhere, rolling in from the ocean wastes and encircling the clear-cut outlines of the red lava-peaks which project from the floor of that vast crater."

After a day and a half of riding horseback to Maui's Haleakala Crater, the above exclamations (and much more) flowed from the pen of the 1890's traveler, John R. Musick. Haven't we all felt the marvel of this unique volcanic landscape?

Mr. Musick was so enthralled with the clouds, cinder cones and cliffy ruggedness that he apparently failed to observe the gorgeous silverswords that were then abundant. An enthusiastic contemporary, however, Isabella Bird Bishop, was entranced with them: "... in a hollow of the mountain, not far from the ragged edge of the crater, then filled up with billows of cloud, we came upon... thousands of silverswords, their cold, frosted gleam making the hillside look like winter or moonlight... They exactly resemble the finest work in frosted silver, the curve of their globular mass of leaves is perfect, and one thinks of them rather as... for an imperial table.. than as anything organic."

So ubiquitous were silverswords at these highest Maui altitudes that even up till 1915 thousands were gathered, dried and shipped to the Orient for ornaments. Turn-

129

of-the-century tourists habitually yanked up large plants, playing games by rolling them down Haleakala's slopes like giant snowballs. An old wedding photograph taken somewhere near the summit, displays a wedding party wearing scraggly silversword garlands. Such a scene, hardly beautiful to our more enlightened eyes, not only symbolized an important occasion to them but represented a continuation of an old Hawaiian custom of picking and wearing plants that were known to grow in areas difficult of access. A few years ago an archaeologist from the Bishop Museum, Pat McCoy, discovered silversword leaves intimately associated with ancient Hawaiian artifacts on the Big Island (11,400', Mauna Kea). Apart from this evidence we have no records that silverswords were used in pre-European times.

Much unthinking human desctruction accompanied by heavy grazing and trampling by cattle and feral goats, pushed the silversword to the brink of extinction by the time Haleakala National Park was opened in 1921. Considerable efforts to control goats within the Park, especially recently, have resulted in a remarkable population increase.

Although the names Haleakala and silversword are normally linked, this plant's original range encompassed three Big Island mountaintops too (Mauna Loa, Mauna Kea and Hualalai). Today the Big Island form is extremely rare; the remaining few dozen individuals are temporarily safe within a sheep- and mouflon- protective fence. We must applaud the National Park Service and State of Hawaii for their goat and wild sheep control, public education programs, fencing, propagation and transplanting efforts on both islands over many years, still in effect. Without these, silverswords would be extinct.

Climbing Mauna Kea in 1825, James Macrae, who first brought knowledge of silverswords to the western world, considered it "truly superb, and almost worth the journey of coming here to see it on purpose." Dried specimens of these dazzling plants, sent to Europe, were later christened in Greek, *Argyroxiphium sandwicense,* literally "silversword of the Sandwich Islands" (former name for Hawaii). It is easy for us to jump in our cars and drive up a paved road to see one, but before 1900 such journeys were only for hardy, dedicated souls. Their expeditions, lasting several days, were pursued on horseback over vast uncharted country with few trails. Weather was summery and glary during the day and wintry and windy at night, and on the Big Island there was always the imminent threat of another volcanic eruption! Shelterless nights in rugged lava expanses, wearing inadequate clothing, breathing oxygen depleted air, were generally cold and miserable. Opportunists such as botanist David Douglas helped allay his chilled body by making a "tolerably good fire" from dried silversword leaves and *pukiawe* twigs.

Patches of rosy snow tinted by glorious sunsets, steaming volcanoes, thick layers of fleecy clouds, bags of precious new plants and days of fabulous adventuring, however, overshadowed the physical difficulties involved in such expeditions. Even today the spectacular panoramas afforded by Hawaii's lunar landscapes, and the possibility of seeing the world famous silverswords in bloom are admirable excuses for spending a day or more away from the comforts of home. It is no wonder that Hawaii's National Parks were selected in 1981 by UNESCO as International Biosphere Reserves.

––––––––––––––––––––

In shall never forget my surprise when I learned that a gorgeous plant just like the silversword, but with red flowers instead of purplish-brown, grew in the high mountains of the Canary Isles, west of Africa. I had thought that Hawaiian silverswords were "totally unique".

As we know, words can be misleading, and we all fall into the trap of using words that we forget to define for particular audiences. When referring to plants or animals, "unique" means "found nowhere else", but there are degrees of

"South American silverswords", actually high elevation Andean saxifrages, not at all related to "real" silverswords. Páramo de Chingaza, Colombia.

uniqueness. Approximately 98% of Hawaii's native plants are unique to our island archipelago. That figure is remarkable, unmatched by any other country or island in the world. However, Hawaiian *habitats* are not radically different from other areas. The original plant colonists arrived here by chance, and the environment often modified them, in many cases dramatically, in such a way that many species resemble unrelated plants in other parts of the world. In the Canary Isles, enough environmental conditions at high elevations were similar to Hawaii's equivalent areas, that silversword-like plants evolved in both island groups, although they do not possess a common ancestor.

"Our" silversword, with its symmetrical, inwardly-curving, reflective leaves, is actually quite typical of plants in high elevation regions of Africa, Asia, New Zealand and South America. For example, imagine yourself in the Andes at 14,000'. The clear afternoon light bounces off thousands of silversword-like rosettes atop their woody stalks which thickly dot the alpine meadows. These beautiful, woolly plants, even though in a different family from silverswords, have adapted to the windswept, desert-like mountains of South America, just as our silverswords have done in Hawaii.

Areas in which silvery-rosetted plants grow, although isolated geographically, share a number of climatic conditions. Have you ever wondered why you get more sunburnt up on Haleakala or Mauna Kea than down at the beach? The reason is that at high elevations the sun's radiation is more intense than at the coast. As we drive higher we move beyond a curtain of clouds, dust and gases that normally protect our skin from strong ultraviolet and other light rays. Above 7,000' plants such as silverswords and silver geraniums respond to this brilliant radiation by producing thick layers of hairs on their leaves. These hairs, together with trapped air (which is responsible for the silvery color) simulate a highly reflective metallic surface such as a space blanket. They not only shield the plant from the drying effects of sun and wind, but act like a mirror reflecting away the brightness (see also page 150). So great is the reflective capacity of large numbers of silverswords that one man on the Big Island recalls how "his eyes glared in the morning sun" when he was above 9,000' in silversword habitat on Mauna Kea. That *was* a long time ago!

Hawaiians called several species of silver alpine plants *ahinahina* or just *hinahina*. As they were not familiar with metallic luster, they appropriately chose its closest equivalent: silver-gray hair.

Silversword rosettes dot cindery puu, Haleakala Crater, Maui.

C. Kepler

As I recall my first encounter with a silversword, the predominant thought in my mind was an amazement that such striking beauty could emerge from this hard, exposed, desert-like environment where hardly anything else grew! With loose cinders, strong winds, daily temperature extremes of heat and cold, precious little rain and virtually no humidity, it seemed miraculous that seeds could even germinate. I need not have worried. Silverswords (and their counterparts in other alpine regions) have had, in general, millions of years to perfect their design and ensure survival in such rugged terrain. Camels of the plant world, silverswords, like cacti, deal with their water problems so well that they can afford to spend up to 20 years in cinders before even sending up a flower stalk!

We have already mentioned the hairy leaves and their obvious advantages to the plant. The perfectly symmetrical rounded rosette obviously is important too, especially considering that so many alpine plants are similarly shaped. Essentially the curving leaves, compactly arranged, act like a "living bowl", catching water and directing it downwards to a central root. The lower portions of the leaves, the most hairy, trap water and air, thus protecting the delicate growing tip deeply seated within the rosette.

The silversword's leaves, as well as being silver, possess straight margins and are narrow. These characters did not happen by accident. Leaves must have a certain area in order to photosynthesize (produce food using sunlight, air and water), but for an alpine plant, the more this area can be minimized the better, as water is lost through the leaves. Stiff leaves also help protect plants from strong winds. Shape is just as important to a plant as it is to a violin.

Within the cells inside these leaves a toothpaste-like gel develops, a bit like but in less volume than, aloes. This thick substance stores water and imparts a succulent turgidity to the leaves. During droughts the silversword can utilize this stored water, causing the plant to droop, but it can still live for months more without rain. Also typical of rosetted plants are the dead basal leaves which act as mulch, preventing lower leaves and roots from desiccating.

Such adaptations have enabled this "grandchild" of a little Californian coastal daisy to enter a large, hostile living space. How different it has become from its ancestor! And how different even are the silversword's Hawaiian relatives! Who would have suspected that the silversword's "brothers" and "cousins" would have chosen not only alpine wastes, wet and dry forests and soggy bogs, but the wettest place on earth, Mt. Waialeale on Kauai?

Scientific Name: Argyroxiphium sandwicense
Other names: ahinahina, hinahina, silversword
Family: Compositae or sunflower family; about 13,000 species; related to daisies, marigolds, dandelions, artichokes, Eke Silversword, *kupaoa.*

Eke Silversword, only two feet high, an inhabitant of a few high elevation Maui bogs.

C. Kepler

The author with a five foot high silversword, Haleakala Crater, Maui. Beauty from dry cinders.

C. Kepler

Beauty from squishy bogs; small Eke silverswords.

K. Kepler

High elevation, bog-dwelling greenswords have lost their silvery sheen.

Greenswords dwell in almost perpetual clouds.

Gentle colors of the greensword's daisy blossoms.

K. Kepler

C. Kepler

C. Kepler

T A R O

K. Kepler

One of many varieties of red-stemmed taro.

Black-stemmed taro (variety hapu'u, *after black and green treeferns).*

Ono kahi ao luau me ke aloha pu kekahi. "A single roll of taro top is delicious if seasoned with affection". It is not the gift that is prized but the way it is given.

In every age and culture virtues involving generosity and love are cherished. Often too, we find that those who are poorest materially have the kindest hearts!

Eking out an existence in old Hawaii was hard. Life was simple and to our present concepts, boring, especially the food. Taro, cherished cargo in the canoes of the first adventurous settlers of Hawaii and still the staff of life in the islands when our first European voyagers arrived, was, however, one of the few commodities always available and ready to be shared. It was the equivalent of rice to Orientals and corn to Mexicans.

Early accounts indicate graphically the impoverished existence of Hawaii's common people. For them, taro (pounded and fermented into poi) formed the bulk of every meal, often with little else except boiled taro leaves (*luau,* from which the feast name was derived), *limu* (seaweed) and periodically a small helping of protein. Steward (1839) tells us that "the poverty of many of the people is such that they seldom secure a taste of animal food, and live almost exclusively on *kalo* and salt", and Douglas, an early botanist, relates his stay with an elderly lady who "compelled her dog to swallow Poe by cramming it into his mouth, and what he put out at the sides, she took up and ate herself." (Recent anthropological research indicates that when white man first arrived, Hawaii's land was overpopulated and there was not enough food for everyone.)

Fortunately taro, although not providing a completely balanced diet in itself, is most nourishing. Nutritional studies show that it supplies many ingredients (such as iron, calcium, phosphorus, Vitamins A and C) necessary for the growth and maintenance of healthy bodies, normally supplied by fruits and vegetables. No scurvy (due to lack of Vitamin C), for example, was observed by early voyagers; in fact, the only signs of scurvy came from the ship's crews!

From an early age, children were taught the meticulous art of preparing poi. Peeling the corm ("root") with a large *opihi* (limpet) shell, steaming it in the *imu* (underground oven), cleaning implements, pounding with a heavy rounded stone, and

fermenting the resultant semi-liquid mass were the main steps in this process. One had to know exactly how much water to add so it would not become soft and mushy. But then one didn't want it to become hard either, otherwise it would turn lumpy and grainy. One of the rules was that children had to eat their first efforts at poi-making – *A timeless scene, Hanalei Valley, Kauai.* wise training to ensure smooth, tasty food!

Every portion of the plant was utilized: the outer skin for plant fertilizer, the scrapings for chicken and hog feed, and the watery residue for massaging babies etc. In some regions, overfermented, stale poi was kept and used, even if it tasted like vinegar. "Waste poi today and tomorrow you may want some and not get it" was a lesson hard-learned by many a family.

"Real" Hawaiians, even today, love poi. It was (and still is) standard fare for babies, children and adults alike. A water-lover like rice, taro is generally grown in "paddies" called taro patches (*l'oi*) bordered by solid earth embankments. Upland taro, grown as any other vegetable, also exists but is less popular. A ready producer of mutants, taro naturally developed more than 300 varieties over many centuries, about 80 of which are extant today. All take from six months to a year to mature.

Each variety differed slightly in its stalk color and height, leaf color and size, and root-type. Red, yellow or black stems (in some cases accompanied by beautiful red or purple leaves) characterized the more unusual varieties. Of paramount importance in agriculture, naturally, was the starchy root; slight variations in glutinosity greatly affected the final texture, taste and keeping qualities of poi.

Taro's large, attractive, arrow-headed leaves lend a picturesque, timeless quality to cultivated farmlands such as Hanalei (Kauai), Waipio (Big Island) and Keanae (Maui), the principal areas for raising commercial taro today. Gardeners at Waimea Arboretum (Oahu) and Keanae Arboretum (Maui) maintain excellent displays of both common and unusual varieties of taro for visitors and residents to admire. Note the imaginative names given to these varieties, indicating the old Hawaiian's familiarity with local plants and animals: a black-stalked, green-leaved taro is *hapu'u* from its resemblance to treeferns; a stripey-stalked taro is *manini* from its similarity to the striped reef-fish; and spotted-leaved taro is *'elepaio,* recalling the prominent white dots on this little bird's wings.

Incidentally, many of today's farmers utilize traditional methods as much as possible: they even move stones to divert the trickling stream water instead of using concrete pipes.

Fresh poi is manufactured daily in the islands and, along with Samoan imports, is a popular item in country stores and supermarkets alike. But poi is not for everyone! Famous (infamous?) for its "library paste" consistency, it has borne the brunt of many a joke. Not only does it *taste* like bookbinder's glue to many Western palates, it has actually been *used* for glue on numerous occasions! Missionary Albert Lyons humorously writes in 1840: "I remember well when wallpaper was first brought to Hawaii. Here was a new art to be mastered. The paste was easy – poi, of course.''

Since that time, poi has prompted experimentation in diverse culinary fields. For example, two Honolulu bakeries in the 1930's carried on a flourishing business baking (apparantly delicious) taro bread, and one hotel long ago offered "poi cocktails" (actually poi milkshakes, complete with ice-cream and vanilla) to curious tourists.

Seriously though, taro symbolized a deeply spiritual facet of Hawaiian culture. Regarded not only as the progenitor of the entire human race, but as the actual embodiment of Kane, the source of all life, it represented prosperity, fertility, long life and the fulfillment of all hopes and desires. From a tiny taro *keiki* growing in the muddy earth sprang man's precious life. By the sun and rain this life was nurtured, and to the earth it returned.... basic facts of life.

References to taro's cultural importance became scattered throughout language and social concepts of the ancient race. For example: *'ohana,* today meaning "extended family" orignally was a term relating to the group of tightly knit, bulbous suckers growing in concentric fashion around the parent plant, each eventually budding off to live an independent life. And, on a lighter note, the taro's *piko,* a little rounded depression where the taro stalk meets the leaf surface, extended its meaning to include man's "belly-button".

Revered and tended with great care during every phase of its growth, taro inspired elaborate religious rituals to ensure that the great gods would continue their blessings. Taro-cultivation in Hawaii rose to the greatest heights of excellence that have ever been known. Today some Hawaiians, in order to retain their cultural identity, have chosen to become taro farmers. Whatever his profession though, an Hawaiian is always honored to share poi with stranger and friend alike, and we are honored to form part of a living link with the past when we partake of it.

> *"O Kane-of-the-living-waters!*
> *Here are the first fruits of our taro.*
> *Return, O god, and grant us food!*
> *Food for my family,*
> *Food for the pigs,*
> *Food for the dogs.*
> *Grant success to me. . .*
> *In farming, in fishing, in housebuilding –*
> *Until I am bent with age.''*

an ancient Hawaiian harvest prayer.

Scientific Name: Colocasia esculenta
Other names: Taro, *kalo, pa'i'ai* (dried, baked taro), *luau* (taro leaf), *'oha* ("root" bud) *huli* (cutting for planting)
Family: Araceae or arum family; about 1500 species; related to calla lily, *'ape, Monstera, Philodendron, Dieffenbachia, Caladium* (popular houseplants).

T

I

Ti: *reminders of long-gone people who baked its roots for a precious sweetener.*

A young Hawaiian lass dips her wooden calabash into the clear, crisp mountain stream and carefully carries it back home to her ailing grandmother. Her family's thatched hut, surrounded by many gracefully plumed *ti* plants, is well-equipped to ward off evil spirits. Before entering the low doorway she lops off a few of these leaves (*la-i*) with a bamboo knife, and tucks them under her arm.

Once inside she severs their rigid portions and submerges the broad leafblades in the stream water. Soon her ageing *tutu* sighs gently as the cold leaves, bandaged around her head and resting beneath her back, provide pleasant relief.

Today many *kama'aina* (old-timers) still cool their paining heads and backs with *ti* leaves. So do I. I think they work better than towelling, as the wax-coated leaves do not absorb body heat as fast as woven cotton cloths. After only one application the refreshing coolness remains with you for quite a while, and works even better if repeated. Try it for a child's fever too; if necessary, wrap his or her entire body in the leaves and change when necessary. Your child may look like a forest elf but should complain less!

Other traditional uses of *ti* included the treatment of coughs, internal hemorrhage, inflamed tissues and various infections, including VD (was this effective?) *Ti*, not at all related to the beverage "tea", belongs in the lily family. This may seem surprising, but botany is full of surprises. Next time you see one in flower, notice

K. Kepler

Ti *leaves: a fine substitute for plastic bags, foil and Saran Wrap.*

its tiny lily-like flowers which are so numerous and delicate they remind you of a gracefully curving spray of orchids.

Although its original home has not yet been determined, *ti* was a valuable plant throughout the Pacific and was carried by Polynesians everywhere they traveled.

Although many people associate this plant with "ancient hula", the famous *ti*-leaf skirts, I regret to relate, did not originate in Hawaii! Truly authentic Hawaiian hula skirts were woven from *hala* leaves and tapa (bark) cloth. *Ti*-leaf skirts were created in the late 19th Century by immigrant Gilbert Islanders who came to toil in Oahu's sugar-cane fields.

Ti, however, was important culturally to the old Hawaiians. It played a major part in the evolution of *kahili* (royal standards), today a familiar symbol of bygone days.

The process had humble beginnings. Break off the bunchy top of a *ti* plant and you have an excellent fly-whisk or fan, necessary items in the days before garbage-collectors and air-conditioning! This fly-whisk soon became an important symbol of truce between warring parties. A messenger, running between chiefs, would announce the cessation of battle by bearing his *ti*-leaf "flag" aloft like a *kahili.* As years progressed, long attractive feathers (mostly from seabirds) replaced the green leaves, and shiny polished handles (carved from wood, whale ivory or turtle shell) replaced the long stalk. Thus, from lowly plant inception, elaborate *kahili* evolved into works of art, carrying considerable status for Hawaiian chiefs (see drawing on page 139).

Simultaneously, the royal feather cloaks and helmets also became more intricate, enhancing a chief's power and enlarging his sphere of influence. This refinement of royal regalia was an obvious development, considering the traditional symbolic value of *ti* with respect to high rank and divine power. *Ti* was especially sacred to the gods Lono (the god whom Captain Cook was assumed to represent) and Laka (Goddess of the hula). Early travelers in Hawaii described how huts dedicated to Lono were bordered and thatched with *ti* leaves.

In the days before plastic bags and refrigeration, *ti* leaves were indispensible items for the average Hawaiian. Their uses were legion, primarily centering around food preparation and storage, but also including such diverse items as sandals, raincoats, medicines, fishing accessories, plates, temporary thatching and toboggans.

Their shiny, waxy leaf surfaces, their large size (commonly two feet long and seven inches wide), their ability to keep foods cool and protected, and their abundance both in the wild and in cultivation, rendered them in constant demand. Anyone who has lived in Hawaii is familiar with the tasty juiciness of *laulau,* standard fare at *luau* (feasts). Pieces of meat or fish are wrapped in *ti* leaves and cook slowly in their own juices. No disagreeable flavor is absorbed from the vegetable wrapping.

The general popularity if *ti* leaves extended until quite recently, when you could buy bundles of them at any general store or fish-market. Today several farmers, mostly on the Big Island, grow *ti* commercially for sale to florists. Such activities take you back to when life was simpler and people lived off the products of land and sea. There is an old saying which refers to the proverbial generosity of Hawaiians: *Hawaii palu la'i.* Loosely traslated, it means: "The people of Hawaii will give away all the fish in their bundle and merely lick the *ti-leaf* wrapper themselves."

Now that's aloha spirit for you!

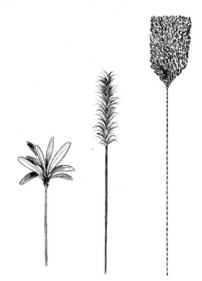

Left to right: ti-leaf fly whisk or banner, simple kahili, complex kahili.

Canoes aren't always used for paddling. In the late 18th Century, soon after Captain Cook visited Hawaii, a certain William Stevenson (an escaped convict from Sydney, Australia), taught Hawaiians an unconventional use for canoes-and *ti* plants that had far-reaching consequences throughout the Pacific.

Prior to the arrival of white men, Hawaiians had brewed a relatively harmless "beer" of low alcoholic content from enlarged *ti* roots. When baked in an *imu* (underground oven), these roots, although fibrous and pulpy, tasted sweeter than sugar cane. After cooking, the roots were macerated with stones in a canoe and left to ferment for six days. At this stage it was rather an unsightly aerated mass, attracting hoards of insects but nonetheless consumed heartily.

Stevenson however, taught the Hawaiians how to further refine this "beer" into an extremely potent, whisky-like liquor which later enjoyed esteemed recognition by the liquor trade. Distillation was effected by an iron try-pot (in which whale-blubber had been boiled!) erected over a fire, with an attached gun-barrel to reduce and draw off the *okolehao*.

The origin of the word *okolehao* (or affectionately "oke") is interesting: *okole* comes from the name for the bottom of the cauldrons, which were shaped like human buttocks, and *hao* means iron. *Okolehao* was both the rig and its product.

Immediately this liquor was a success. A veritable "gift from heaven", everyone became addicted to it: white men (sailors and ship's captains) and Hawaiians (commoners and royalty). It was many years, unfortunately, before King Kamehameha noticed its devastating effects upon himself and his subjects. *Okolehao* and *'awa* were largely responsible for the pathetic assemblage of drunkards so often mentioned in accounts by early Hawaiian missionaries.

Actually European diseases (such as VD and measles), coupled with excess consumption of *okolehao* were highly instrumental in decimating the large populations of Hawaiians in the 19th Century. Fatal repercussions from these regrettable influences were felt throughout the Pacific, reaching as far away as remote Pitcairn Island, lonely refuge of the "Bounty" mutineers. Here a crude *okolehao* still, adapted from a British teapot, resulted in incalculable agony and death.

Ships visiting Hawaii in the early days customarily procured large quantities of

K. Kepler

Ti *leaves made fair raincoats too.*

ti for their long voyages; its roots provided "beer" and *okolehao,* while the leaves served as livestock fooder. These alcoholic beverages provided welcome adjuncts to the sailors' meagre rations of "grog" (rum). Tremendous quantities of *ti* plants were gathered during this period of intense exploitation. Some stands never recovered.

Many of Hawaii's **kaamainas** remember *okolehao.* During Prohibition those exceptionally fond of it paid up to $100 a gallon! By that time distillation was more refined, utilizing Portuguese grape-wine stills, copper coils, siphons and oak barrels. I'm sure that residual grape flavor tasted better than residual whale-blubber flavor too!

Even now in back-country valleys one occasionally runs across large patches of *ti* that obviously represent former contraband *okolehao* operations. Just as today young fellows will hike miles to tend *pakalolo* (marijuana) plants, similarly men not too long ago would go to no end of trouble to maintain their "secret patch".

During famines, huge quantities of *ti* roots were gathered from nearby forests and baked in communal ovens, Such sweet treats were uncommon additions to an otherwise quite bland diet, relieved by pieces of sugar cane, sweet potatoes and a few native berries.

William Ellis, an early missionary, frequently boiled *ti* roots into a sugary syrup. Chemically this sugar is related to sweeteners in sweet potatoes and honey. It was produced in prodigious quantities by each plant; some roots weighed over 30 lbs!

Such strong and enormous roots must have been difficult to pull up without the aid of iron gardening tools. The effort involved must have prompted the following proverb: *"Pull hard at the ti roots, my brother, and you will live. Be strong and courageous." Ti* itself is also practically indestructible. Even if destroyed by a storm, its large amounts of stored underground energy allow it to survive and sprout forth anew.

In our present age of rapid changes, both in the world and in ourselves, let us resolve to be strong like the *ti* plants, drawing on our internal reserves of energy and strength.

Scientific Name: Cordyline terminalis or *Taetsia fructicosa*
Other names: Ti, ki, la'i (contraction of *lau-ki, ki*-leaves)
Family: Liliaceae or lily family; 2,800 species; related to dracaenas, Easter lilies.

140

R. Hobdy

K. Kepler

Wauke's leaves are coarse, sandpapery and shaped like those of kukui.

A representative valley where you might be lucky enough to find wauke.

WAUKE
(paper mulberry)

They stared at the fine white "tapa" that Captain Cook's men were showing them. Ah – very fine and extremely white, signs of purity and good bleaching. And how even was its texture! One could scarcely distinguish individual fibers. Its straight blue lines were evenly spaced and the designs, well... they were different but regular and quite intricate.

This white man, the long awaited god Lono, was certainly a superior being. Had they not seen more of his excellent handiwork in those huge white sheets of tapa that caught the winds to move his big ship?

Imagine yourself landing, as the first white men to Hawaii did, amongst people who had no notions of paper, writing, or conveying ideas by means of symbols. In Captain King's own words: "They looked upon a sheet of written paper as a piece of cloth striped after the fashion of our country, and it was not without the utmost difficulty, that we could make them understand, that our figures had a meaning in them which theirs had not."

Tapa: it is a familiar word to anyone who has traveled in the Pacific. Bark from the paper mulberry tree (*wauke*), soaked and beaten, has been cleverly converted into lengths of paper-like cloth here for centuries. Actually the word *tapa* is a corruption of *kapa*, the original Hawaiian term meaning "the beaten thing". (As "k's" and "t's" are interchangeable in Polynesian languages, this is understandable.)

Up till relatively recently there were no native peoples anywhere in the world that were so dependent on the products of a small tree (like *wauke*) for their clothing and bedding, than those inhabitants of far-flung Pacific islands. Woven coconut and pandanus (*hala*) sufficed on hot atolls, but wherever cool winds sprang up and cold mountain air was evident, *wauke* was indispensable for making more flexible attire. Why? Because such islands had no native land mammals from which to secure skins and fur, the standard source of warmth in continental regions. (Hawaii does have a native seal, but its skin was apparantly never used.)

Carried tenderly to Hawaii in pioneering canoes, *wauke* was nurtured as pains-takingly as food-plants. It is a pretty scraggly tree; its leaves are rough and sand-papery, and its fig-like flowers and fruits sparse and inconspicuous. It is just the kind of tree that one walks right past without even noticing! However, using time-tested techniques of bark-stripping, soaking and beating, Hawaiians not only manufactured passable cloth, but rose to exceptional heights in the production of their finest quality colored or patterned material. Tapa grades varied, depending on the island region, bark quality and maker's skill.

A woman's basic attire was a knee-length wraparound skirt (*pa'u*), similar to the *lavalava* and *pareu* worn on other Pacific islands today. Nine-foot long loincloths (*malo*) sufficed for the men, and shoulder capes (*kihei*) were commonly used by both sexes to warm the upper body and arms. Light bed-covers, composed of several layers of tapa, kept many a shivering body cozy on rainy, draughty nights.

One 19th Century traveler, traversing the high elevations on Mauna Kea (Big Island) assured us that five sheets of this local bedding left him uncomfortably warm, even though water was freezing in calabashes at his feet.

Most prized of tapas were the fine yellow and white ones, used by royalty. Tiny, wispy baby shawls and soft flexible loincloths were the softest, produced after endless hours of beating. Skirts, normally only a few feet long, were made in enormous sizes for the *alii* (royalty); one was measured at 130 feet, a staggering dimension when one considers that a good *wauke* branch yields strips only about three inches wide!

The wife of a pioneer missionary, writing of a feast given by King Kamehameha II in 1820, described the queen's dress as a roll of tapa one yard wide and long enough to encircle her body 70 times. To array herself in this unwieldy attire, two attendants spread the tapa on the ground, after which the queen rolled her body over and over until only a bit of tapa was left to tuck in at the side. She must have appeared gigantic!

Black tapas, dyed by burying in taro mud, were also of high quality. Up to 40 pieces have been found wrapped around corpses long ago buried in caves.

Tapa-making in Hawaii ceased around 1890; however, early detailed accounts and descriptions from living persons present to us a clear picture of the skill and work involved. It was important to soak the *wauke's* inner bark strips for just the right amount of time so that their woody fibers would break down and starch would wash away, yet the remaining fibres be tough, resilient and malleable enough to be pounded into a reasonably durable cloth. Naturally each phase of the long operation was attended by prayers and supplications to the appropriate gods.

Ancient Hawaii... one's mind immediately envisions loincloth-clad men beating sticky cooked taro with poi-pounders, and full-skirted women sitting by low wooden "tables" thumping away at tapa cloth. These were the activities that consumed most adult hours. And, just as an Irish knitter can be identified by her sweater patterns, so a Hawaiian woman was known by the characteristic "watermark" that her tapa

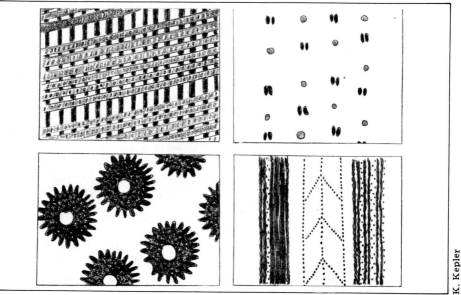

K. Kepler

Hawaiian tapa *patterns (after Brigham).*

beater printed on her tapa.

During the course of centuries, Hawaiians experimented with numerous types of wooden beaters, using different dimensions, different native hardwoods (usually *kolea*) and different carved patterns on their sides (a fern leaf, simple diagonal, duck track symbol etc.). Today the Bishop Museum in Honolulu harbors about 350 different beaters. After imported clothing took over, tapa beaters were not discarded either – they appropriately beat the dirt out of European skirts on washday!

When all the fibers had been rearranged so they were uniform, the tapa was ready to be dyed with natural dyes, imprinted with bamboo stencils, waterproofed with sticky adhesives, and perhaps scented with aromatic seeds and oils. Early accounts leave no doubt that Hawaiian tapa was superior to that in the rest of the Pacific in its variety of color and design, yet was not always of the finest quality with regards texture and degree of waterproofing. Portlock and Dixon (1779) tell us how tapas were "stamped with various colors and diversity of patterns, the neatness and elegance of which would not disgrace the window of a London linen-draper."

Planted extensively on all the Hawaiian islands, *wauke* became sorrowfully neglected after imported clothing became the rage, and today it is quite a rare plant. Unless you like to hike into remote hills and valleys, you will have to be content with viewing it in our major botanical gardens. However, at the Polynesian Cultural Center (Oahu), Tongans daily demonstrate the making and dyeing of tapa, and do-it-yourself craft classes are periodically offered at the Lyon Arboretum (Oahu).

If you look hard, too, you can often see fluffy white tapas spread out to air on the blue floor of the sky. Hina, the goddess of tapa-making, once lived on earth, but, being an overly industrious worker, she once annoyed the great god Tangaroa with her constant mallet pounding, and was consequently relegated to living far away, where she could make all the noise she wanted. Thus her base of operation is the moon, where you can see her face as she beats away and watches lonely voyagers on the ocean below. I don't know her source of *wauke* bark – certainly not Hawaii these days!

Wauke... it is like a botanical Ghandi: beneath a smallish, plain exterior it was once a giant-sized and indispensible contributor to our welfare and cultural heritage.

Scientific Name: Broussonetia papyrifera
Other names: paper mulberry, *wauke, aute* (rest of Pacific)
Family: Moraceae or fig; about 1000 species; related to rubber trees, mulberries, figs.

K. Kepler

A Polynesian cornucopia: wauke, taro, olonā and banana, all miles from the nearest road.

Luxuriant pristine forest, where Polynesian man never ventured to cultivate wauke, bananas or taro.

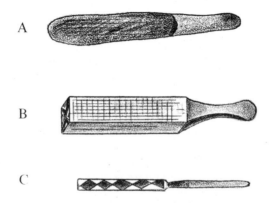

A. First tapa beater, B. Patterned tapa beater, C. Design stencil.

144

W
I
L
I
W
I
L
I

".. like the trunk of the wiliwili
Which was shaped for a surf-riding board."

Hawaiian surfboards, ancient and modern.

Today in Hawaii we take surfers for granted. How often have we heard the expression, "O, he's only a surfer"? How often have we driven by Oahu's north shore and not even bothered to watch the graceful surf-rider on those exquisite, turquoise, curling waves? Surfing is an incredibly fine art, becoming more refined as the years pass. Zipping along inside a dynamic tube of crystal water, riding the steep face of a gigantic wave, and executing sharp maneuvers are a few of the difficult feats in a good surfer's repertoire. For the average enthusiast, practically anything done on a board is exhilirating. Boards these days range from small boogie boards, on which a surfer lies prone, to a bewildering array of larger boards with specializations in shape, size, and fin-type. But is all this recent?

For centuries surfing and other water sports were major Hawaiian pastimes. Their preferred wood for surfboards was Hawaii's native *wiliwili,* a pale wood which approaches the lightness of cork or balsa, even though most people today imagine all old boards were fashioned from *koa,* a much heavier native timber. According to early travelers, Hawaiians were the surfing masters of the Pacific. In Hawaii, the absence of extensive fringing reefs enclosing placid lagoons, and the presence of numerous rocky bays and points, favored the development of waves that do not crash all at once but have the clean, unfolding, unbroken edge necessary for smooth rides. Most other Pacific high islands do not have these coastal conditions.

The Hawaiians rode on both long and short tapered boards, just as we do now. The long boards (*olo*) actually had a range of lengths far greater than those today. *Olo* measured up to 24 feet long, were about three feet wide, and were heavy and cumbersome; some *koa* boards weighed 180 lbs! Obviously light woods were preferred.

The smaller nine-foot boards (*alai'a*), ridden while prone, were the equivalent of today's boogie boards – in fact, our modern shorter designs are based on these *alai'a*! They were constructed principally from breadfruit (*'ulu*) or *koa* trunks.

Surfing similarities do not end here. In olden days, competitions were also held. Dozens of competitors of all ages, and both sexes, vied for winning places, riding towards markers near the shore. Techniques and courtesy were not too important: it was more of a race to see who could get there first. These "meets" attracted great crowds and involved much eating, partying and lasciviousness, according to missionaries. It was common for a boy and girl traveling on the same wave to ride all the way to the beach then terminate their exhiliration with a passionate embrace on the shore! Such behavior, plus the betting of valued possessions (men sometimes rashly bet everything they owned, including their wives), led to the banishment of the entire "wicked scene" for over 50 years. Surfing was not revived until 1910.

Although the missionaries, greatly perturbed by the morals associated with surfing, apparently did not appreciate it as an aesthetic skill, many early voyagers did. They were astounded and often fearful. In 1779, David Samwell, surgeon's mate on Captain Cook's vessels, stated his feelings in colorful, now antiquated language: "The Motion is so rapid... that these people seem to fly on the water, the flight of a bird being hardly quicker than theirs... these People find one of their Chief amusements in that which to us presented nothing but Horror and Destruction, und we saw with astonishment young boys and girls about nine or ten years of age playing amid such tempestuous Waves that the hardiest of our seamen would have trembled of face, as to be involved in them among the Rocks, on which they broke with a tremendous Noise, they could look upon as no other than certain death."

Wiliwili surfboards, although softer and lighter than *koa,* were durable enough to withstand repeated batterings. The Hawaiians, obviously having no shock-cord

Wiliwili *in her summer glory.*

K. Kepler

Large clusters like this bloom for weeks.

leashes, readily abandoned their boards when in danger. Despite this desertion, surfboards were treasured possessions.

Every aspect of surfing was intimately bound with religion. When selecting a *wiliwili* (or other) tree, a red *kumu* (purplish goatfish) was first offered to the presiding deity. Drying and seasoning the wood followed this ritual, then much careful shaping. After the basic form was carved, the board was sanded with increasingly fine corals, then with sharkskin. Finally it was rubbed with a black stain made from *kukui* nut soot, then with several coats of coconut oil. After use, the more fastidious surfers dried their boards thoroughly, oiled them to maintain the glossy finish, wrapped them in tapa cloth and suspended them from rafters in their huts.

Anyone knows that waves can exhibit phenomenal power, even when they look relatively innocuous. To the old Hawaiian, a petition to the source of these supernatural forces was a necessary prelude to entering surf. He needed divine power (*mana*) to control his actions and protect him.

It may be of interest that a common Polynesian belief was that coral trees (of which *wiliwili* is the Hawaiian representative) originated from the churning of the ocean. Is this another reason why they were used in surfing?

Wiliwili also made excellent fishnet floats and canoe outriggers. More recently it has been carved into imitation whale-tooth necklaces (*lei palaoa*).

It is an odd-looking deciduous tree with poisonous sap, which thrives in the hot dry foothills of our islands. Characteristic of rocky or lava-strewn regions up to 1500', it is most easily encountered on Haleakala's south slope (Maui) as you drive from Ulupalakua to Kaupo. Note its short cylindrical trunk, knobbly branches and bright clusters of big, pea-like flowers (red, orange or cream).

When one considers the inherent difficulties in carving an incredibly long board, keeping it waterproof, carrying it to the beach when the surf was up (a car with roof-racks is much easier), and grappling with it in the water without fins or ankle-leashes, it is surprising that surfing was so popular. Yet the Hawaiians loved the sport and were the best in the Pacific.

As David Samwell aptly stated in his concluding remarks about the struggles and successes of ancient surfers, "So true it is that many seeming difficulties are easily overcome by dexterity and Perseverence."

Scientific Name: Erythrina sandwicensis
Other names: wiliwili (refers to the twisting action of seedpods as they liberate
    seeds), Hawaiian coral tree, Hawaiian erythrina
Family: Leguminosae or legume; about 12,000 species; related to peas, tiger's claws.

Wiliwili's flowers come in white too.

Spirally opening seedpods inspired wiliwili's
Hawaiian name.

*It's hard to imagine surfboards coming from
this swollen-trunked, desert-adapted tree!*

K. Kepler

C. Kepler

ABOUT THE AUTHOR

C. Kepler

Dr. Angela Kay Kepler, a naturalized New Zealander, was born in Australia in 1943. Although she holds advanced degrees in marine biology and ornithology, she developed a love for Hawaii's plants and culture when first exposed to the islands as an East-West Center student at the University of Hawaii in 1964. Since then she has lived and traveled on every continent with her biologist husband, Cameron. Together they have hiked and camped extensively throughout Hawaii's mountains and lowlands.

They have authored and illustrated several books and numerous scientific publications, and Kay writes weekly newspaper columns on biological aspects of the Hawaiian Islands.

Kay and Cameron presently reside in upcountry Maui with their two adopted Korean girls (page 91).

K. Kepler

*Ka'u Silversword leaves (*Argyroxiphium kauense*), from Is. of Hawaii at high elevations.*

front cover: *A lobelia (*Clermontia montis-loa*), 4,800', Island of Hawaii. K. Kepler.*
back cover: *Mamane (*Sophora chrysophylla*), 6,100', Maui. K. Kepler.*
inside covers: *Maidenhair ferns (*Adiantum raddianum*), 1220', Molokai. K Kepler.*
title page: *'Ie'ie vine in flower (*Freycinetia arborea*), 1300', Molokai. K. Kepler.*